JULIAN BARNES

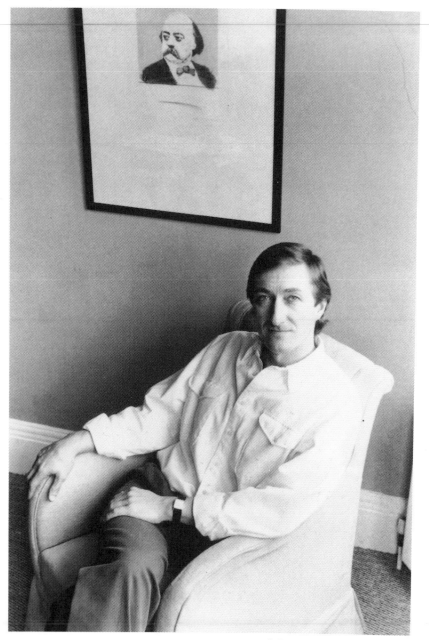

JULIAN BARNES

JULIAN BARNES

MATTHEW PATEMAN

© Copyright 2002 by Matthew Pateman

First published in 2002 by Northcote House Publishers Ltd, Horndon, Tavistock, Devon, PL19 9NQ, United Kingdom.
Tel: +44 (01822) 810066. Fax: +44 (01822) 810034.

British Library Cataloguing-in-Publication Data
A catalogue record for this book is available from the British Library

ISBN 0-7463-0978-3

Typeset by TW Typesetting, Plymouth, Devon
Printed and bound in the United Kingdom by
Bell & Bain Ltd., Glasgow

Dedicated to the Memory of Ruth Elliott
and Doris Pateman
and
The Future of Sophie and Victoria Bird

For Jim Elliott

Contents

Acknowledgements

Despite its brevity, this book has, in one way or another, been in the making for over a decade. In that time, many people have contributed to the life in which the book has been developed. I cannot mention them all here, but especial thanks are due to the following: Kevin Johnson, Hindpal Bhui, Richard Samuels, Claudia Grillo, K. Leach, and Lynne Voyce; all the staff and students at The University of Leeds English Department, 1990–4, especially Richard Brown and Alistair Stead for their scrupulous readings of my Ph.D. thesis; Inga-Stina Ewbank for having faith; Mark Robson, John McLeod, Antony Rowland, Angela Keane, Patsy Badir, and Eriks Uskalis for thought and friendship; to the various staff members at University College Scarborough, now The University of Hull Scarborough Campus, who make working there such a pleasure, particularly Lucy Bending, Fran Brearton, Charles Mundye, Keith Spence, Ann Kaegi, Anna Fitzer, and Catherine Wynne. Thanks also to Isobel Armstrong for remembering me.

Without Martin Arnold this book and my career would never have happened. I owe him and Maria an impossible debt. To my parents, who have been my guides and mentors, what can I say: thank you. And to Kelly, who has had to watch me disappear into the computer screen, and only ever gave me love in return: without you, I'm nothing.

The author and publisher would like to thank Random House UK Ltd for its permission to quote from the works of Julian Barnes.

Biographical Outline

1946	Julian Patrick Barnes born, 19 January.
1957–64	Attends City of London School.
1968	Graduates with Honours in Modern Languages from Magdalen College, Oxford, and begins work as a lexicographer on the supplement to the *Oxford English Dictionary*.
1977	Works as a reviewer for the *New Statesman* and *New Review*.
1979–86	Television critic for the *New Statesman* and the *Observer*.
1980	Publishes *Metroland*, and *Duffy* under the pseudonym Dan Kavanagh.
1981	Receives the Somerset Maugham Award for *Metroland*, and publishes *Fiddle City* as Dan Kavanagh.
1982	Publishes *Before She Met Me*.
1984	Publishes *Flaubert's Parrot*, which is shortlisted for the Booker Prize.
1985	Awarded the Geoffrey Faber Memorial Prize for *Flaubert's Parrot*, and publishes *Putting the Boot in* as Dan Kavanagh.
1986	Publishes *Staring at the Sun*; is awarded the *Prix Médicis* for *Flaubert's Parrot*, and the E. M. Forster Award.
1987	Publishes *Going to the Dogs* as Dan Kavanagh, and is awarded the Gutenberg Prize.
1988	Made *Chevalier de l'Ordre des Arts et des Lettres*.
1989	Publishes *A History of the World in 10½ Chapters*.
1991	Publishes *Talking It Over*.

1992	Publishes *The Porcupine*, and is awarded the *Prix Femina* for *Talking It Over*.
1993	Awarded the Shakespeare Prize by the FVS Foundation.
1995	Publishes *Letters from London*, and is made *Officier de l'Ordre des Arts et des Lettres*.
1996	Publishes *Cross Channel*; the film *Love etc.*, based on *Talking It Over*, is released, dir. Marion Vernoux.
1997	The film version of *Metroland* is released, dir. Philip Saville.
1998	Publishes *England, England*, which is shortlisted for the Booker Prize.
2000	Publishes *Love, etc.*
2002	Publishes *Something to Declare*.

Abbreviations

BSMM   *Before She Met Me* (London: Jonathan Cape, 1982)
EE   *England, England* (London: Jonathan Cape, 1998)
FP   *Flaubert's Parrot* (London, Jonathan Cape, 1984)
HW   *A History of the World in 10½ Chapters* (London: Jonathan Cape, 1989)
LE   *Love, etc.* (London, Jonathan Cape, 2000)
M.   *Metroland* (London, Jonathan Cape, 1980)
P.   *The Porcupine* (London, Jonathan Cape, 1992)
SS   *Staring at the Sun* (London: Jonathan Cape, 1986)
TIO   *Talking It Over* (London, Jonathan Cape, 1991)

1

Introduction: 'The songs were the man ...'

As a Ph.D. student, I wrote to Julian Barnes asking for help with my thesis. He replied promptly. He sent me a postcard of Arundel tomb, two figures side by side, carved out of stone and emphatically not alive. On the other side he had written 'While I am glad you are reading my books, being studied and researched makes me feel like this', at which point an arrow indicated the lifelessness of the picture. I suspect that this polite rebuke was based partly on a suspicion that Barnes may have thought that I was going to be more interested in the writer than the writing.

Barnes has been fastidious in his refusal to allow his work to be used as a biographical or psychological tool in the analysis of him. A comment from his account of the year 1981 written for the twenty-first anniversary celebration of Picador publishing makes the point clearly. Although discussing Jacques Brel, the implication for Barnes himself seems unambiguous: 'The songs were the man; any biography was unimportant, reductive.'[1] He has stressed that, while *Metroland*, his first novel, has a 'spirit' and a 'topography' that are autobiographical, the 'incidents were invented'.[2] Even when there appears to be a claim for authorial presence, as in the 'Parenthesis' section of *A History of the World in 10½ Chapters* or the last line of the collection of stories from *Cross Channel* ('And the elderly Englishman, when he returned home, began to write the stories you have just read'[3]), these are always playfully undermining of the possibility. And, as I mention later, he baulks at the idea that his work constitutes an *œuvre*.

1

So, this book is not about Julian Barnes. This book is about the novels that carry the name 'Julian Barnes'. As such, there is a quantity of work that will not be discussed, which includes his journalism and short stories, his reviews (televisual, literary, and culinary), his translations (*The Truth about Dogs*, a German cartoon book, being a sad omission), and his four detective novels written under the pseudonym Dan Kavanagh. Aspects of these are discussed in Merritt Mosely's *Understanding Julian Barnes*.

Barnes's last two novels to date look back on his earlier works (with varying degrees of explicitness and success) and this provides the pattern for discussion in the present volume. I have attempted to treat each of the first seven novels as a discrete production, eschewing an idea of progression or development. The last two chapters, in some measure, act as an overall survey as well as providing accounts of the novels in question.

Despite the claim for 'novelty' in each book, there are concerns that do recur in Barnes's novels, among which are male friendship, sexual fidelity, obsession, betrayal, love, the status of knowledge. These are allied with a formal dexterity that means each novel seeks a new mode of storytelling, a new direction for narrative. Indeed, it is partly this formal ingenuity that has assured Barnes's novels their status, especially, perhaps, *Flaubert's Parrot* and *A History of the World in 10½ Chapters*.

The dazzling diversity of Barnes's books is not simply a modish whim. Each book, in its different ways, is asking us to reconsider how we view the world, and this consideration is both formal and thematic – assuming that the two can be bifurcated like that. Barnes's novels are all searching for ways of knowing the world, each other; they all have characters who are striving for some way of finding meaning in an increasingly depoliticized, secularized, localized, and depthless world. From the political quietism of Chris in *Metroland*, to the insane biologism of Graham in *Before She Met Me*; from the quiet despair of Braithwaite in *Flaubert's Parrot* to the substitution of facts for wisdom in *Staring at the Sun*; from the failure of history in *A History of the World in 10½ Chapters* to the relativism of the present in *Talking It Over*; from the clash of ideologies in *The Porcupine* to the death of ideology in *England, England* to the striving for mythic possibility in *Love, etc.*, Barnes's novels are a catalogue of the desire for, and the failure to find, a purpose beyond bland being and a position from which judgements can be made. As with the postcard I received, Barnes's novels offer a polite rebuke to the platitudinous relativism of postmodern culture as well as to the failed pieties that no longer serve. Often regarded as witty and clever, Barnes's novels are also subdued melancholic meditations. Detached and ironic, they are also softly passionate. Caught between the Beckettian pessimism of waiting 'for nothing to happen' (*LE* 250) and the attenuated belief of 'Such hope!' (*SS* 111), the nine novels written by Barnes since 1980 all ask the reader that they, like the novels, engage in 'trying to find new certainties in a moral vacuum'.[4]

2

Starting out in Paris and London: *Metroland*

Deceptively simple, *Metroland* is the prize-winning first novel that signalled a new and important talent on the British literary scene. Intelligent without being brazen, witty without being glib, international at the same time as being parochial, emotionally full and distantly cool, *Metroland* modestly proclaimed itself and its author as a force to be reckoned with.

Told in the first person by Chris, the story is in three sections. The first has Chris in Metroland in 1963 as a clever 16 year old. Section Two moves to Paris in 1968. The final section is back in Metroland in 1977. Each of the sections is fronted by an epigraph and a brief, prefatory, unchaptered introduction. This triptych-style organization allows for a number of ideas in the story to be indicated at the level of structure. First there is a certain ambiguity concerning the narrative: should it be thought of as a simple linear tale moving through time, or should it be thought of as a circular movement, as a returning to beginnings? Secondly, the epigraphs suggest a reading that sees the story or the narrator as becoming less and less interested in searching, in striving for truth, in uncovering symbols. This, in turn, indicates the importance of art and its shifting functions for Chris as the tale unwinds. This relates to questions concerning the relative merits of French and British writers, of France and Britain in general, ideas of masculinity involved in both sets of cultures, and this returns us to the movement of the narrative and Chris's seeming complacency as the novel progresses.

Christopher seems to be a model of creeping quietism; sliding from the pose of radical young questioner to a complacent early-middle-ager. His lifelong friend, Toni, the other major character for most of the novel, represents a macho leftism that seems redundant and cynical rather than a useful antidote to the simplifying desire of Chris, a simplification first indicated by his changing attitude to art.

It is with art that the novel opens. Chris and Toni are standing in the National Gallery watching the visitors through binoculars. The point of this exercise is explained a little later by Chris:

> (Art) made people not just fitter for friendship and more civilised (we saw the circularity of *that*), but *better* – kinder, wiser, nicer, more peaceful, more active, more sensitive. If it didn't, what good was it? Why not just go and suck cornets instead? *Ex hypothesi* (as we would have said, or indeed *ex vero*), the moment someone perceives a work of art he is in some way improved. It seemed quite reasonable to expect that the process could be observed. (*M*. 29)

Art for the young Chris should be revered because it is ennobling, improving; Chris sees art as hope, redemption. By the end of the novel, though, the adult Chris has lost this belief.

This illustrates the main movement of the book: the decline from 'coruscating idealism' (*M*. 15) to 'sold out' adult (*M*. 167). The seeming complacency of the older Chris is less marked than it was in the initial drafts of the novel, where he was 'amazingly complacent' in a manner that 'was just wrong for that kind of time structure' according to an interview with Ronald Hayman.[1] This decline is marked meta-textually by the epigraphs that open each section. These are taken from Rimbaud's oblique symbolist poem 'Voyelles', Verlaine's brief discussion and explanation of that poem, and Bishop Butler's exhortation to accept surface meanings and reject the unnecessarily complex and symbolic. There is a movement from complexity to simplification, from the desire to search to the desire to accept.

Chris's urge during the course of the novel is to simplify, to reduce meanings, to stem the proliferation of signification that he had once found so exciting. It is to this desire to accept, to simplify, that Chris has sold out by the end of the novel: 'there's no point trying to thrust false significances on to things . . .' (*M*. 176).

The young Chris, in the section opened by Rimbaud's 'Voyelles', sees the world as a place open to interpretation, to aesthetic enquiry: 'At that age everything seemed more open to analogy, to metaphor, than it does now. There were more meanings, more interpretations, a greater variety of available truths. There was more symbolism. Things contained more' (*M.* 13). Chris and Toni believe that by stripping away the confused layers of meaning you could find 'stuff like the purity of language, the perfectibility of the self, the function of art, plus a clutch of capitalised intangibles like Love, Truth, Authenticity . . .' (*M.* 15). By the end of the novel, Chris is happy to accept things. He is unwilling even to engage in ironized aesthetic symbolism: 'I follow a half-factitious line about the nature of light: how the sodium with its strength and nearness blots out the effect of even the fullest moon . . . and how this is symbolic of . . . well of something no doubt' (*M.* 176).

Between the searching Chris inscribed by Rimbaud and the sold-out Chris inscribed by Bishop Butler's exhortation to keep to surfaces and appearance ('Things and actions are what they are, and the consequences of them will be what they will be; why then should we desire to be deceived?'), there is the transitional Chris. This is the Chris caught between the superabundance of meaning and symbols, and pragmatic conservatism. He is inscribed by Verlaine: 'Moi qui ai connu Rimbaud, je sais qu'il se foutait pas mal si A était rouge ou vert. Il le voyait comme ça, mais c'est tout' (*M.* 73). For this Chris, symbols still hold sway, but their meanings are limited and personalized. At his first meeting with Annick, who will become his girlfriend, the many nuances and cadences of their conversation denote multiplicity, but go no further than self-awareness, self-construction. Having previously attempted to scour away the proliferating signs of society, the mythologizing spectre of the natural, he begins to take an active role in social semiotics. Recognizing the power of the image, he succeeds in seduction via signifiers. He is very aware of, if slightly hesitant about, this process:

All this may sound cynical and calculating; but that wouldn't really be doing me justice. It was, I liked to think (perhaps still do think), more the result of a sensitive desire to please. It was as much a matter of how I imagined she would like me to appear as of how I would like to appear to her. (*M*. 93)

The fusion of symbolism and solipsism is most forcefully felt in a passage from the central section of the novel. Having kissed Annick for the first time, Chris sits down in the garden of the Palais Royal. Imbued with a sense of history, culture, and the weight of received symbols, he is very much aware of the *now*, of his presence and relationship to everything:

> The past was all around; I was the present; art was here, and history and now the promise of something much like love or sex . . . and bringing it all together, making it mine was me – fusing all the art and the history with what I might soon, with luck, be calling the life. (*M*. 93)

This passage draws together all the central elements with which the later novels will be concerned to varying degrees: love, history, art, and, with Chris as the nexus, the novel also focuses on ideas of identity, and the relationship between personal and public narratives.

The movement to simplification that is Chris's progress is marked strongly when he visits his favourite gallery, the Musée Gustave Moreau. Describing Moreau's work, Chris explains his delight in the paintings; it is because they contain 'that odd mixture of private and public symbolism which at the time I found so beguiling' (*M*. 107). This is Chris's meridian. After this point, anything that suggests multiplicity, circumlocution, or lack of straightforwardness is ignored by him. It is as though he has tired of looking below the surface.

While Chris might eschew the delight of interpretation, the reader has no choice. This can produce its own problems, as Frank Goodman's undelighted review illustrates: 'A novel that lapses into foreign words, phrases and quotations irritates me.'[2] The novel's emphasis on the need for the reader to translate, to interpret, is most evident in the need for translation from French into English: Rimbaud and Verlaine; the occasional one-liners; the rhyme 'Le Belge est très civilisé' (*M*. 15); and most pointedly in Chris's relationship with Annick in Paris. Here, of course, the burden of translation is also on Chris's shoulders and not just the reader's. For Chris, it is not

7

simply the rendering of one phrase into a different tongue, but the negotiation of a culture as experienced through its language. As well as highlighting translation as an essential part of the novel, the discussion surrounding language also forms a major strand in the novel's questioning of character, history, love, and truth.

By highlighting translation as a literal activity, the novel has created in Christopher a highly unreliable narrator. The text's foregrounding of possible interpretations that the narrator does not offer produces a tension that is compounded by Chris's almost wilful betrayal of his earlier beliefs. The older Chris, thirty-something, married, and happy, tells the reader: 'But I've given up – I think – half-truths, just as I've given up meta-communication: wonderful in theory, but unreliable in practice' (*M*. 140).

The narrator does not meta-communicate, so where do the epigraphs (meta-communication at its most obvious) come from? If they are supposed to be Christopher's idea, then he is now, most patently, not telling the truth. If, though, they are intended to be distinct from the narrator and are an authorial imposition at a meta-textual level, then we are being informed by the narrator that the author (or, at least the author's techniques) cannot be trusted. The idea that Chris's slide to simplification can be reduced to the meaning of the novel, that *Metroland* can be read as symptomatic of a postmodern decline, is to ignore the complexity of the novel's narrative structure.

Our perception of the teenage Chris's personality is as much influenced by the descriptions of the books he reads as by his actions. His version of himself is heavily indebted to his idealized view of the 'sophisticated tough' (*M*. 16) as exemplified by Camus and Henri de Montherlant. The apparent rigour and strenuousness of French writers appeal to Chris's desire for the pure, the solid, and lend credence to his own pedantry and seriousness. Added to which, the French seem to Chris to have an endless supply of women about whom he and Toni can fantasize.

Narratorially, Chris offers the reader aspects of his personality via the literature he reads and the importance this holds for him. The possibility of seeing character as being constructed through literary engagement is made most explicit in *Flaubert's*

Parrot, both with Braithwaite's own ruminations and with the introduction of the Mauriac game. Beyond the purely literary, this and later novels also demonstrate the ways in which character is created in and through language. There is too the further investigation of the ways in which character is determined by and helps to determine the broader social and cultural contexts in which the individual lives.

It is not just the highlighting of writing in general that allows for these ideas to be displayed, but the pointed marking of this as the writing of a first novel. Not everybody appreciated the fact of the novel's clear position as a 'first novel'. In a typically scathing piece, Auberon Waugh castigates the fact that Barnes is 'far too old to be writing a First Novel'. More than this, Waugh, with beguiling condescension, suggests that 'Mr Barnes's real purpose . . . is not so much to write a First Novel as to review the First Novel he might have written if he had written one (like the rest of us) at the age of 18'.[3] Be that as it may, through a weaving of narrative ploys, the novel relates its own position as a first book to ideas of social status, sexual inexperience, voyeurism, and, through a conflation of all of these, to the nature of narrative and thence to questions of subjectivity and history.

In Paris, he loses faith with the symbolic possibility of this aesthetic, and a world view it might be thought to uphold to a degree. Here, he seems more interested in sex and a self-absorbed notion of history. His history, however, is remarkably abstracted from the events taking place around him: it is more of a formal mechanism than an attempt at understanding: 'You always need to shove at least one big date (1789, 1848, 1914) into your title, because it looks more efficient and flatters the general belief that everything changes with the eruption of war' (*M.* 83). So entranced is he by the formal that the real seems to have disappeared from his sight:

> 'Absolutely fucking typical. Only time you've been in the right place at the right time in your whole life, I'd say, and where are you? Holed up in the attic stuffing some chippy . . . I suppose you were mending your bike during that skirmish of 14–18? Doing your eleven-plus during Suez . . . And what about the Trojan wars?'
> 'On the lav.' (*M.* 77)

9

The point is not that Chris missed out on *les événements* (the uprising in Paris in May 1968) but that he does not care that he did. The history either embarrasses or bores him. He becomes lax and imprecise about his time there: 'Oh, late Sixties' (*M*. 75). History, if it is uncomfortable, is best forgotten by the postmodern Chris. But nostalgia is something to which he can cling with precision and joy – the date of his loss of virginity is recorded exactly: 25 May 1968. The slightly vaguer 'May '68' has a corresponding loss for him: the loss of history.

This is shown more forcefully in the final section of the book, 'Metroland (1977)'. Two signs notably unmentioned are Queen Elizabeth II's Silver Jubilee and the explosion of youthful anger that was punk. Books, once the promise of so much for Chris, are now his workaday business; gimmicky coffee-table tomes that look like what they talk about – even the books can be judged by their covers for him now. He is aware of his own position, of his substitution of nostalgia for history, of the surface, the cover for what is hidden underneath, but is perfectly able to accommodate these ironies: 'isn't part of growing up being able to ride irony without being thrown?' (*M*. 135).

The place where history still does reside is Toni. But his cynical, macho leftism appears crude, reductive, and impotent. Despite this, though, he still retains the anger and curiosity that Chris has lost. While Chris is riding the irony of going back to an old-boy school reunion, Toni is not so easily seduced. Chris replies that Toni is not exactly Rimbaud himself, but the sadness behind this comment is revealed when, talking of the Symbolists, Chris says: 'But what do these complaints urge, except pointless excess and disloyalty to one's character? What do they promise but disorientation and the loss of love?' (*M*. 174). The heroes have become the whipping boys in Chris's slide to simplification and the rejection of history. And all apparently in the name of love.

The first of the 'capitalized intangibles' that the young Chris and Toni are searching for is Love. He finds this abstraction in Marrion and Annick. What Chris prizes most about Annick and Marion, though, is their honesty – and this begins a quest for a link between love and truth that finds its zenith in the 'Parenthesis' section of *A History of the World in 10½ Chapters*.

He remarks: 'Previously I had – even with Toni – been honest for effect, competitively candid. Now, though, the effect may have been the same to the outside observer, inside it felt different' (*M.* 100). Chris feels more honest, responds to Annick with honesty, and attains an understanding of what Truth is: 'a simple inward glance' (*M.* 101). Truth, in the reflected glow of love, becomes nothing more difficult than self-contemplation. However, as Chris is to discover, things are more complicated than that. He becomes confused about his feelings for the English woman, Marion, whom he has met in the Moreau. The first description of Marion says 'her manner, though quiet, seemed direct' (*M.* 108). And it is her directness, her straightforwardness, which appeals most to Christopher. Her questions raise complex and differing emotions in Chris, but she is honest, she speaks the truth. A concern of a number of critics with regard to the women characters in Barnes's novels is articulated early on by Bernard Levin, who is worried that the 'directness and truthfulness' of both Annick and Marion are the only real characteristics of the two.[4]

Back in Metroland in 1977, Chris's quest has all but foundered, 'Things and actions are what they are . . .' and states of mind can be reduced into lists and the softened language of contentment, 'feeling as if we had shares in everything' (*M.* 134). Love, Truth, Authenticity have dwindled into metaphors of monopoly, prefiguring Stuart's claim in *Talking It Over* that love and money are analogous systems.

Truth is offered to Chris uncompromisingly when, in a conversation over infidelity, Marion says:

'you may as well know that the answer is Yes I did once, and Yes it was only once, and No it didn't make any difference to us at the time as we weren't getting on perfectly anyway and No I don't particularly regret it, and No you haven't met or heard of him.' (*M.* 163)

Marion does not capitalize the intangibles of Love, Truth, and Authenticity but the certainties of Yes and No. And it seems that Chris prefers the certainties to the hazy intangibles. He delves no deeper, seeks no further explanation or self-examination. He simply moves himself further away from the examination of truth.

11

Throughout the novel Chris has moved away from his original ambition. Symbolism is replaced with surface acceptance; history is first appropriated and then forgotten; love declines to a shopping list; and language becomes progressively less and less trustworthy. Beside Chris's simplification, Toni represents the idealist fomented into cynic, espousing a doctrine seriously damaged in Paris in 1968 and appearing to be a brutal, insensitive, and ultimately selfish response to Chris.

One justifies his life by the pragmatic acceptance of comfort and irony, the other by looking to a system whose credibility is strained to breaking point. The text does not offer us any choice between the two.

3

The History Man: *Before She Met Me*

Before She Met Me, inevitably perhaps, suffered from comparisons to its Somerset Maugham Prize-winning predecessor. There was a sense that the novel was both too ambitious and too slight. The theme of jealousy had been done better elsewhere (Angel Clare, Othello, and, most damagingly for some critics, in *The End of the Affair* by Graham Greene), and the characters were too flimsy and unattractive to bear the weight of the story. Mark Abley was especially disappointed in the novel, particularly when compared to Greene's work: 'one has only to remember the passion, tenderness, complexity and moral seriousness of Greene to realize something of what's lacking in *Before She Met Me*'.[1] Barnes's novel, however, is not just a reworking of the theme of jealousy but is also an examination of one of the main debates arising from modern science: the extent to which individuals are constructed by their environment or their genetic make-up.

Graham Hendrick, the paranoic main character of *Before She Met Me*, is a history lecturer at London University. He is married to Barbara, has a child with her, falls in love with Ann at a party hosted by Jack Lupton, a writer friend of his, and then becomes increasingly jealous of Ann's life before she met him. This jealousy is not just what Graham describes as the 'natural wish-I'd-been-there wistfulness' (*BSMM* 115) of most lovers but an uncontrollable and violent obsession related specifically to the films that Ann had appeared in, and the possible permutations of on- and off-screen affairs that she may have had with the leading men.

That Graham is a history lecturer and Jack is a fiction writer allows the novel the scope to interrogate the conception of history as so many versions of narrative (within, it must not be forgotten, a fictional narrative form) and to interrogate ideas concerning identity and madness.

The first piece of text that the reader encounters within the covers of the book (after the author biography, the title page, and publishing history) is a quotation taken from the *Journal of Nervous and Mental Diseases*, 135/4 (October 1962):

> Man finds himself in the predicament that nature has endowed him essentially with three brains which, despite great differences in structure, must function together and communicate with one another. The oldest of these brains is basically reptilian. The second has been inherited from the lower mammals, and the third is a late mammalian development, which . . . has made man peculiarly man. Speaking allegorically of these brains within a brain, we might imagine that when the psychiatrist bids the patient to lie on the couch, he is asking him to stretch out alongside a horse and a crocodile.

This quotation, which is documented as in a textbook, locates Hendrick within a strongly materialist conception of the self – a conception where the self is given (or at least heavily determined by) biological and neuro-physiological factors. This is set up in the novel in the form of questioning the degree to which the brain is controller or controlled (a theme made explicit when Graham worriedly wonders: 'What if your brain became your enemy?' (*BSMM* 132)). The structure and capacity of the brain also provide a working metaphor that becomes the title of the last chapter: 'the horse and the crocodile'. What is of interest here is the fact that the narrator has decided to give his readers the reference for the quotation, allowing them, should they so desire, to check it for accuracy and fidelity. During the novel, Hendrick uses a whole host of archival material, but their accumulation is secret and their uses are dangerously abstracted from their original context.

The next piece of text is a little quotation from Molière's *Les Fourberies de Scapin*: 'Il vaut mieux encore être marié qu'être mort'. This quotation sets up the themes of linking notions of marriage with death. What these two quotations serve to do is create a relationship between the scientific and the aesthetic.

Whether this relationship is one of oppositionality (hierarchized in favour of one or other of the categories or not), or whether it is one of mutual interdependence, is not obvious. It remains the case, however, that a relationship is being offered to the reader to ponder.

With these two quotations, the narrative is also opening up a variety of different expectations and, as in *Metroland*, it is asking the reader to engage with the text as an area of fluidity and translation while also making him or her aware that the possibilities are not limitless and that the boundaries of the text are real if not distinct (that is, this is a piece of fiction quoting self-consciously from a piece of non-fiction and another piece of fiction) – a state of affairs that Hendrick, from within the confines of the novel, is not allowed to recognize.

The use of quotation and archive in the novels under discussion comes to the fore in *Flaubert's Parrot, A History of the World in 10½ Chapters*, and, in a different fashion in *England, England*, but its use in the body of the novel in *Before She Met Me* is also interesting. Jack, Hendrick's writer friend, is a flamboyant larger-than-life character (similar in his capacity as foil for the straight man to Toni in *Metroland* and Oliver in *Talking It Over* and *Love, etc.*) whose use of archive reflects how archival use is as much a character as a thematic trait in the novel. He markedly exaggerates the findings of the Kinsey Report in order to make a point to Graham about the fact that it is fine to masturbate and more or less ad libs a theory of Koestler's, again to try and reassure Graham as well as simply enjoying the process of knowledge and exaggeration (*BSMM* 73).[2] It is apparent, however, that this is as much a character trait of Jack's as it is a narratorial investigation into the possibility of verisimilitude. When Graham is reading to Ann from one of the books he has picked up on holiday in France, his quotations are faithful to the original (*BSMM* 102). Despite the fact that one of the passages is slightly misquoted – the word 'when' is used in *Before She Met Me*, whereas the original translation has the word 'while' – the implication is that the attempt to be faithful to the source and not to misrepresent or mis-read it is being made.[3]

This is in sharp distinction to the ways in which Hendrick uses the archival material at his disposal when trying to piece together Ann's life. Importantly, the first stirrings of his jealousy and, consequently, of his perversion of the archive and history, are created by the cinema. As a history lecturer, Hendrick has always been a 'words man' (*BSMM* 118), not greatly affected by the visual. Indeed, one of the initial causes of his attachment to his first wife, Barbara, was their mutual dislike of the cinema, so much so that 'Not going to the cinema had been one of their first observable characteristics as a couple' (*BSMM* 26). The degree to which one's conceptual apparatus may shift is one of the main concerns of the novel, as indicated by the quotation at the beginning and also by Graham's response to the loss of some holiday snaps. For the purposes of the present discussion, it is the ways in which Graham uses his new-found cinemaphilia that are of greater importance.

He has gone to the cinema in the first place because his first wife has said that their daughter wants to go and see a film that features her school. This is not the case and the entire trip has been set up by Barbara in order to embarrass him in front of his daughter, as she will see Ann playing 'a tart' (*BSMM* 30). While this most certainly does happen, and Ann herself recognizes this as the primary motivation behind the scheme, it is the effects on Graham that are the most astounding.

He asks Ann if she slept with the leading man, Dick Devlin, and she replies that she did. Her directness and honesty appear to make this the end of the matter, and, as with Annick and Marion in *Metroland*, the relationship between straightforwardness, truth, and love is again broached. However, the affair is not at an end. Graham becomes obsessed with the film, and others in which Ann appeared. He goes to see Jack to discuss his worries, especially his fear that Ann has slept with all the leading men. Jack's commentary is linked by the narrator to the concept of a narrative:

> he'd been fairly convinced by the plot structure he'd presented to Graham at such short notice. He'd managed to impose some sort of pattern on both their lives as he went along. Still, that was his job, after all, wasn't it: smelting order out of chaos, rendering fear and panic and agony and passion down into two hundred pages and six quid ninety-five. That was what he was paid to do, so this wasn't too hard a sideline. The percentage of lying was about the same as well. (*BSMM* 49)

16

After having been to see Jack, Graham becomes less and less capable of deciding what constitutes a narrative, of locating the barrier between life and fiction. He and Ann are discussing where to go on holiday; Arezzo seems a possibility until Graham remembers that Ann has been there with Benny, one of her previous boyfriends. Ann is mildly pleased at the memory, 'jarred by pleasure at the thought that she had been doing interesting grown-up things for such a length of time . . .' (*BSMM* 53). Graham, on the other, has a much more specific memory to play with:

'You went to the cinema in Arezzo,' said Graham slowly, in the tone of one prompting a child, 'and you saw a bad sentimental comedy about a whore who tries to disgrace the village priest . . . and then you went back to your hotel and you . . . screwed Benny as if you would never know greater pleasure, and you held nothing back from him, absolutely nothing, you didn't even save a small corner of your heart and leave it untouched for when you met me.' (*BSMM* 54)

Graham admits that he has invented the last part of his story, but the conviction with which it is recounted illustrates the beginning of an obsession that will lead him over the edge of sanity. Apart from the places where Ann has not been, the only possible locations left to Graham's jealous mind are those places where Ann has had her period. The whole issue of menstruation is one of fascination for Graham (as indeed it had been an area of perplexity for Chris in *Metoland*).[4] It is explained that Barbara saw her period as 'a time when women's suffering should be exalted, when she should be allowed an extra degree of irrationality in decision-taking' (*BSMM* 106). Graham's attitude to the discovery of periods can be related to Ann's open-mindedness about her body, but the emphasis on this aspect of biology has an important thematic element. Pondering the apparent difference between women's and men's spatial awareness, Graham asks himself, 'Was it all conditioning . . . or brain structure?' (*BSMM* 57). Graham's eventual decision is that he is the subject of biological destiny. Despite this though, Graham is set on course for a thorough re-creation of biography and history and he is not averse to nurturing nature to suit his own ends.

17

The holiday time has been a relief for Graham and Ann from the growing irrationality of his jealousy. On their return, however, he starts to search the house for evidence of Ann's infidelities, but 'Sometimes he wasn't sure what constituted evidence . . .' (*BSMM* 59). In the absence of any sure knowledge of what might be considered, of what might reasonably be called Ann's sexual archive, everything becomes open to scrutiny. A walnut box of foreign coins represents, for Graham, a fresh release of disappointment every time a new currency is come across, as this illustrates one more country that Ann went to without him and, more importantly, with somebody else. Her collection of matchboxes presents him with similar possibilities, lets him play the same 'game' (*BSMM* 59). The matchboxes do provoke a degree of uncertainty, as Graham cannot be totally sure that Ann actually went to the places that are displayed because he knows that her friends give her boxes from wherever they go in order to boost her collection. With a deft piece of irony it is stated that 'There was no point in getting jealous unless you were accurate about it . . .' (*BSMM* 60). He also rummages through her book collection, but he does so in such a way that the random search for evidence becomes systematized in a morbid parody of a child's game:

> He had to find the books on Ann's shelves which had been given her by other people. If he didn't find one such book in four tries, he lost the game. If he got to one on the fourth go, he had another turn; if he got one after only two goes, he saved himself two goes, and so had six chances in the next round. (*BSMM* 60)

The destructive search for evidence, however frantic and misrepresentative, has up until this point remained in some arena that could be called real. The currency, the matches, the books, even the films do exist as objects in the real world that Graham inhabits. He is guilty of over-emplotment (as with his narrative about Benny in Arezzo) and over-determination (a particular coin is necessarily an index to a man's name rather than a country's) but not of outright invention. Now, though, his obsession becomes so great that the boundaries between the real and the imaginary become blurred.

Graham has continued seeing films in which his wife appeared, as well as films in which the men she acted with appear, even if she does not. After going to see one of these films, 'the sneering dreams began. The dreams which were so strong, and so contemptuous, that they strode carelessly across the barrier of consciousness' (BSMM 80). These dreams revolve around a common theme that is Graham being told by an assortment of different leading men how many times, and in what manner, and with how many other people present, they have had sex with Ann. In themselves these dreams are not surprising, but Graham adds them to the store of archival material that he can use against Ann. There is no admission of the different realms of consciousness or validity that his dreams have. In one of these nightmares Larry Pitter, a cockney wide-boy, welcomes Graham as Mister Carwash because Ann in this dream had enjoyed group sex, which 'she said . . . was just like being in a carwash' (BSMM 89). The next day Graham is uncommonly happy for no apparent reason until he drives past a garage with the sign offering different products. The last item on the list is a carwash (BSMM 91). Graham's day is shattered. Each garage he drives past he peers at the signs. If 'carwash' is not on one he feels elated. The completely coincidental lack of the sign disproves his fears of adultery, but when the word does appear they are all recon-firmed, re-enforced. A mixture of a dream and the sporadic appearance of a word on a billboard is now all the evidence Graham needs to prove his wife's unfaithfulness. His ethical judgements are being worked through an aesthetic creation. His historical narrative is a montage of disparate forms, his self is an auto-generative self-fulfilling bricolage.

Later, Jack, during a typically facetious piece of advice, identifies Graham's problem. Graham, by allowing almost everything into his archive of proofs against Ann, has lost his sense of discrimination. What he needs is to have no archive (BSMM 121). This advice has no impact, and Graham becomes more and more obsessed, vengeful, and intolerable to be with. Ann decides on a party as a relief, as a gesture that things are manageable. She does not invite any old boyfriends, naturally, but she does have to invite Jack. She has told Graham that she and Jack never had an affair, but they did. The affair had lasted from the autumn of 1972 to the summer of 1973, with a couple of brief liaisons after this. Ann apologizes to Jack for rewriting his past and he replies that it is all right as he is always doing it himself. While this may appear to be the same as Graham's construction of a biography that ignores the possible validity of the referent, it is quite different. Graham's construction is a total fabrication, an arbitrary narrative threaded between disparate states and forms that he believes to be true: he invents his own referent. Ann and Jack, on the other hand, have no such confusion about the status of their affair. It happened and, because it happened, and because of Graham's state of mind, there is a real risk of a trauma as a result. They knowingly lie. They recognize the referent, accept its truthfulness, and attempt to make sure that the *truth* is not discovered by Graham.

They have not counted on Graham's capacity to invent, however. After an innocuous incident at the party between Jack and Ann, Graham begins to compile the dossier of their infidelities. Having 'discovered' the relationship, Graham thinks he knows exactly where to look for the necessary proof. Jack uses what are described as 'tributes and dues' (*BSMM* 149). These are little cameos of friends or enemies who appear in Jack's novels. Graham, therefore, looks in Jack's novels to see where Ann might turn up. Fiction and biography, criticism and mania, merge: Graham finds his proof. With such a capacity to discover evidence from his over-determined vantage point, it does not take long for Graham to assemble a pile of pages that 'added up to half the length of a late-period Lupton' (*BSMM* 153).

Graham heads off for Jack's house. On his way, he returns to the neurological theory, believing that the only real difference between what people believed in the Middle Ages and now is that the metaphor of blood, liver, and bile has moved up to the head. But the fact remains that it is 'the offal that came out on top' (*BSMM* 161). The 'horse and the crocodile', the two less developed layers of the brain, which Jack had likened to 'one layer of Four-Eyes, two layers of Sawn-Offs' (*BSMM* 77), are in control. All that one can do is accept defeat.

The absolute recourse to a materialist explanation is seen to be as hopeless and as damaging as the claim that we are completely divorced from our bodies and capable of creating ourselves as a work of art. Neither theory allows for anything other than resignation or a euphoric complacency. In Graham's case, the choice is for a resigned acceptance of what he sees to be the natural narrative conclusion of his predicament. The fact that this narrative has been effectively self-made does not occur to him.

Ann discovers his secret dossier of her 'life': cinema reviews, film times, photos, adverts, and the extracts from the novels. She also watches a video of a TV ad that features one of her ex-lovers. Taking the signs for what they are, an obsessive and mistaken biography of herself that implicates her in an affair with Jack that has been going on all the time she has been married to Graham, she rushes round to Jack's house, lets herself in, and goes into Jack's room. She follows Graham's stare to Jack's dead body and is then led into the kitchen where her arms are tied behind her back as she faces the garden window. Graham then sits down and cuts his throat open. He had not expected Ann's next action, which is to smash her head through the window and scream for help, but he is dead by the time the emergency services arrive.[5]

Hendrick has proposed a biologically determined view of the individual, but has practised an extreme form of self-invention through narrative. Neither position has enabled him to cope with his despair and obsession. Barnes's next novel, *Flaubert's Parrot*, has a narrator who seeks his relief from despair through an obsessional relationship with a dead writer.

21

4

Seek, Memory: *Flaubert's Parrot*

Since its publication in 1984, *Flaubert's Parrot* has become the most written about of Barnes's novels. Almost universally acclaimed, the most surprising fact about the novel is that it did not win the Booker Prize. Not surprisingly, the aspects of the novel focused on by most critics were its formal ingenuity, depth of research, and breadth of knowledge. These, when related to the questions provoked by this research, were very well received by critics.

The book's tangential and seemingly discontinuous narrative form has led a number of critics to question the novel's status as a novel. The blurb on the jacket sleeve called it a 'book', not a novel, and the American publishers Knopf subtitled it 'a novel (in disguise)'. The disguise has been variously labelled as: 'trans-generic prose text' by J. B. Scott, 'part novel and part something else' by Richard Brown, and 'palimpsestically constructed' by R. Todd.[1] It is certainly the case that the organization of the novel poses problems in relation to the linearity of narrative, but it is also true to say that linearity still persists even if the form in which it exists is an attenuated one. Braithwaite's quest is to discover the true parrot, the one that Flaubert really used as his model for Loulou. This desire to know, absolutely, is also evident in the subtext of his quest, which is to comprehend the suicide of his wife and to learn to cope with his loneliness. He is searching for truth, security, and coherence. It might appear strange, then, that his method of striving for these goals is through contradiction, chaos, and disorder.

The narrative content, if one is to view it as being solely Braithwaite's search for the parrot, is often discontinuous with itself, or only tangentially relevant. If, however, one is to view the parrot's importance in relation to narrative as a structural as much as a content figure, then the narrative can be recognized as both discontinuous and linear. The parrot in the text, after which Braithwaite is questing, is an illusive and elusive creature – impossible to locate or identify exactly and, as such, situated within the thematic argument of doubt, contextual provisionality, and representational formulations. The parrot is an overdetermined symbol, which can be seen by the number of possibilities afforded it in the novel. As a structural feature, however, its function is more precise. The discovery of the two parrots in the first chapter and the subsequent search for the real parrot is not dealt with seriously again until the final chapter, where the search is concluded although not resolved. The structure of the novel, therefore, is disrupted but nevertheless completed within the traditional mode of solving a riddle or puzzle. Andrzej Gasiorek has likened the novel to 'an intellectual whodunnit', an idea supported by Maria Vaizey, who called the book a 'kind of detective literary story'.[2] Following the likes of Vladimir Nabokov and Umberto Eco, this novel uses the genre model to interrogate the possibilities of both literature and knowledge. The fact that Barnes is an adept writer of detective fiction, as seen in the 'Duffy' novels, seems to suggest a certain authorial playfulness in this intriguing perversion of the genre.

The puzzle – detective paradigm is the case even if the intervening chapters have upset the expected causal choices. Where the reader might have expected a continuation of Braithwaite's exploits in the second chapter, he or she is presented with three chronologies of Flaubert's life. By addressing the life of Flaubert, the chapters are linked, if only tangentially, in terms of the story, and by demonstrating the degree of knowledge that Braithwaite has about his subject, character development can be seen to have occurred, even if it is only the implication of an obsessive relationship between narrator and dead writer. Thematically, also, the ideas of indeterminacy and conflicting, but equally viable, facts are here glaringly illustrated.

The quest of the narrator, Geoffrey Braithwaite (to discover which of the two parrots claimed by their owners to have been the model for Loulou in Flaubert's *Un cœur simple* is the real one) leads him to question the very possibility of knowledge: 'Demand violently: how can we know anybody?' (*FP* 155). This urgent desire of Braithwaite to *know* (the parrot, Flaubert, his wife, himself) is constantly undermined by contradictory evidences, a state of affairs in which the reader also finds him or herself. The reader, though, has the added complication of trying to know the novel, its curious form, and its narrator. The question of the narrator, or, more properly, the extent to which the narrator is the same as the author, was posed by a number of critics. John Gross refers to 'Braithwaite (or Barnes)', Bernard Génies suggests that 'M. Braithwaite, pardon, M. Julian Barnes nous tient par le bout du nez', D. A. N. Jones says 'Dr Braithwaite – or Julian Barnes . . .', and Michael Wood has Barnes hiding ' discreetly behind Braithwaite'.[3]

There are three episodes in the novel where Barnes's relationship with his narrator is particularly interesting. The first two simply serve to demonstrate the dangers of assuming any sort of direct correspondence between writer and narrator, of trying to secure a reading of the novel through recourse to author biography. The third episode demonstrates the ways in which the relationship between writer and narrator can be interesting in the effect it has on the stability of the text and on the narrator.

The first two episodes are related to Braithwaite's accounts of literature, the first to do with Flaubert, the second with the Thirties poets. When defending Flaubert against the accusation *'That he teaches no positive virtues'* in 'The Case Against', Braithwaite berates what he calls the 'tactical hypocrisy' (*FP* 133) of some defence counsels in obscenity trials. In response to the question of whether a book is sexy or not, Braithwaite rejects the answer 'No, M'lud, we hold that it would have an emetic, not a mimetic, effect on the reader' in favour of the response 'M'lud, we bloody well hope so' (*FP* 133). This position is very similar to the one espoused by Barnes when reviewing a book about the making of Monty Python's *The Life of Brian*. In response to the charge that the film was blasphemous, the defence was that it was not, and, even if it were, then true believers should have enough faith not to be worried by it.[4] Braithwaite and, in this instance, Barnes would prefer the reply, 'For Christ's sake, M'lud, the matter's as clear as the loincloth on the Crucifixion' (*FP* 133).

It would be wrong to mistake this congruence as some sort of proof of author–narrator identicality. As part of Braithwaite's version of the Mauriac game, which will be discussed presently, he states his dislike of 'the Auden–Spender–Isherwood crew (preaching socialism as a sideshoot to homosexual law reform)' (*FP* 97). Here Braithwaite's views and language are very similar to those expressed by Waugh in his *Essays, Articles and Reviews*. This book was reviewed by Barnes and heavily censured by him for Waugh's espousing of these ideas.[5] The extent of the discontinuity between writer and narrator was spelt out by Barnes in an interview with Jean-Pierre Salgas. When asked by Salgas if he shared Braithwaite's opinion of these poets, Barnes replied 'j'aime beaucoup Auden, Spender et Isherwood'.[6]

An episode that is more interesting in terms of the creation of narratorial voice is that in which Braithwaite is lamenting the poor state of Flaubertian scholarship. He mentions having read a recent novel in which the narrator discusses 'the first, suppressed edition of *Madame Bovary*' (*FP* 78). As Braithwaite goes on to point out, there was no first, suppressed edition of this novel and suggests to the author that he sort this anomaly out in time for the second edition. The book about which Braithwaite is talking is, of course, *Metroland* by Julian Barnes. At its simplest levels what we have here is an author creating a narrator who chastises the author for a mistake in which a previous narrator said something factually inaccurate. This has the effect, for the reader aware of the reference, of disturbing the realms of the real and the fictional.

At the same time as further disturbing the possibilities of the novel, this reference has the effect of securing Braithwaite's legitimacy as a narrator. This is the case to the extent that Braithwaite's knowledge of his ostensible object of study, Flaubert, is recognized as being expansive and detailed. His role as narrator–biographer is, therefore, enhanced. Further than this, though, is his awareness of the responsibility of the narrator to his readers. He excuses William Golding's mistake about the type of lenses Piggy would have had to have in order to make a fire in *Lord of the Flies* as an 'external mistake' (*FP* 77) that would hardly be noticed (as with the mistake in *Metroland*) and that, even if it were, would not 'set fire to other parts of the novel' (*FP* 77). What he is less ready to excuse are 'internal mistakes', when the writer claims two incompatible things about his own creation (*FP* 78). The reader then is presented with this almost as a statement of intent, that Braithwaite will be as accurate and honest as he can be.

This desire to be truthful and accurate is bound up with a knowledge of how form can influence the information given. His search to identify himself is evident throughout the text but is most explicit in his discussion of lonely hearts advertisements. Braithwaite offers us his own: '60 + widowed doctor, children grown up, active, cheerful if inclined to melancholy, non-smoker, amateur Flaubert scholar, likes reading, food, travel to familiar places, old films, has friends, but seeks . . .' (*FP* 95). As he goes on to say, this précis, while not actually lying, is not telling the truth either. The writer of the advertisement is forced to conform to its rules, its norms, and, therefore, to proffer an image of himself that, owing to its mono-discursive nature, is a static representation:

> Two conclusions: first, that you can't define yourself directly, just by looking face-on into a mirror; and secondly, that Flaubert, as always, was right. Style does arise from subject matter. Try as they might, those advertisers are always beaten down by the form; they are forced – even at the time they need to be candidly personal – into an unwished impersonality. (*FP* 95)

To seek to discover an identity via a single discourse or a straight mimetic relationship with a projected image, leads, in fact, to a flimsy monolith devoid of personality or selfhood rather than ensuring a firmly grounded, securely centred self

Braithwaite's preferred mode of seeking identity is 'the Mauriac game' (*FP* 97). He declines to play because he does not consider himself to be of great enough 'importance' (*FP* 97), although it would appear to the reader as if the entire Flaubertian discussion is simply one very focused version of Mauriac's *Mémoires*. In those memoirs, Braithwaite tells us, Mauriac finds himself by looking at the works of others. He defines his own faith by a passionate anger against Gide the Luciferian. Reading his 'memoirs' is like meeting a man on a train who says, 'Don't look at me, that's misleading. If you want to know what I'm like wait until we're in a tunnel, and then study my reflection in the window.' (*FP* 96)

Braithwaite's identity as presented through his autobiographical narrative is partially derived from reflections and deferral as described above. There are occasions of direct communication about himself, however, and these tend to be when discussing his relationship with his wife who committed suicide. In 'Cross Channel' Braithwaite gives us his clearest explanation of his motivation for writing:

> Three stories contend within me. One about Flaubert, one about Ellen, one about myself. My own is the simplest of the three – it hardly amounts to more than a convincing proof of my own existence – and yet I find it the hardest to begin. My wife's is more complicated; yet I resist that too . . . Ellen's is a true story; perhaps it is even the reason I am telling you about Flaubert instead. (*FP* 86)

The story about Ellen that he finds difficult to start is not particularly an effort to understand her causes for suicide, as these seem to Braithwaite to be fairly self-evident and are all predicated on her inability to provide convincing answers for herself in response to the question 'Why go on?' (*FP* 166). He recognizes the futility of feeling self-reproach at her death, of asking if there was any way he could have stopped her: 'Did I try? Of course I tried. But I was not surprised when the mood came upon her' (*FP* 166). While the suicide of Ellen is a great sadness for him, Braithwaite's main reason for writing about Flaubert is not to try to understand her death but to try and come to terms with the loneliness that it is causing him now. He expands upon the notion of loneliness with explicit relation to the death of a lover: 'Lovers are like Siamese twins, two bodies with a single soul; but if one dies before the other the survivor has a corpse to lug around' (*FP* 169). The designation of himself as a lover, as having existed within a loving relationship, is vital for his capacity to articulate himself as a subject and also provides a further level of structural complexity in the novel's disparate narrative.

Despite his emphatic insistence on the category of lover, Braithwaite has a plural notion of what the conditions of love might be: 'Or perhaps her concept of love was simply different; why do we always assume it's the same for everyone else' (FP 162).

Braithwaite also seems to accept a notion of love that does not need reciprocity: 'I loved her; we were happy; I miss her. She didn't love me; we were unhappy; I miss her' (FP 162). Both of these statements can be true without disturbing the position of loving subject that Braithwaite has assumed. In trying to understand his loss, Braithwaite needs to understand Flaubert; in order to understand Flaubert, he feels he needs to understand the parrot. The parrot, that is, along with the other symbolic roles attributed to it by Braithwaite, becomes a symbol of metonymic identification. The discovery of the second parrot swiftly reprimands this easy metonymy, 'The writer's voice – what makes you think it can be that easily located?' (FP 22). Structurally, as has been stated, the 'parrot-quest' chapters begin and conclude the novel, creating an enclosed chain, a love-quest narrative.

This love-quest narrative is dominated by Braithwaite's attempts to know Flaubert, to discover as much about him as possible, to construct him. This construction is based upon an archive that is drawn together by Braithwaite in an attempt to create the man and to provide him with an understandable historical context.

In *Flaubert's Parrot* archive is being used by Braithwaite to form an image, a biography, of Flaubert. This biographical endeavour draws Braithwaite into some speculations about the nature of historical recording and writing. Both of these activities, however, it should not be forgotten, are predicated on the need for Braithwaite to try to come to terms with the loneliness caused by his wife's death. In other words, the uses to which the archive is being put are determined, and go beyond an investigation of history as being simply one further form of fiction. History, though, whether fictional or not, is an impossible entity to enclose or subdue, being as it is 'a piglet which ha(s) been smeared in grease', 'a bare wooden perch', 'a distant receding coastline' (FP 14; 60; 101).

If, though, Braithwaite's attitude to history is that it can never be wholly identifiable, then why is his use of archive so expansive and exact? Partly the answer can be seen to lie in the notion of Braithwaite's narrative as a process of self-identification from within which he can create a stable interpretative context for himself, and also stable interpretative contexts with which to talk about Flaubert and Ellen.

It is his desire to be able to understand his relationship with Ellen and his relationship with himself that necessitates the construction of these contexts; a construction that presupposes a purpose for the subsequent judgement – even if, for Braithwaite, that judgement is generally damning.

Part of Braithwaite's efforts to create a context of interpretation through an archive revolves around a grouping-together of objects that provide him with a physical and immediate contact. These old objects and relics, as well as offering a direct relationship with the dead writer, also serve (as one might have expected in this consistently contrary book) to have an opposite effect, which is that of making the biographer faintly ridiculous in his own eyes: 'I frequently had to get down on my hands and knees to squint in to the cabinets: the posture of the devout, but also the junk-shop treasure-hunter' (FP 20).

The parrot is a member of this set of contextual markers, as the earlier-mentioned metonymic identification shows, but it is also a member of other sets. It works, ironically, as 'Pure Word' and, as such, parody of the writer who is no more than a 'sophisticated parrot' (FP 18). It is what Flaubert created her as being; a symbol for the Holy Spirit in Un cœur simple. It is Braithwaite's metaphor for Flaubert in 'Louise Colet's Version': 'the parrot, the parrot in gloves' (FP 151). This is in addition to the parrot's significance structurally as narrative unifier.

Apart from physical objects, of which the parrot is the prime example, that constitute the archive, the most extensive body of material used by Braithwaite to create the archive are written works. It is primarily through texts that the construction of Flaubert is made, and these texts, with the significant exception of the supposed correspondence between Juliet Herbert and Flaubert, are verifiable. The allusions or quotations are often referenced by Braithwaite, but even when they are not there is always the potential to check their veracity.

The use of Flaubert's correspondence is faithful to Steegmuller's translations of the letters, both in explicit reference and in unattributed allusion. To provide evidence for all the references would necessitate quoting a substantial portion of the novel, so I shall simply provide one example here. The third section of 'Chronology' is made up entirely of extracts from Flaubert's letters to different people. Against '1846' there is an entry that is clearly derived from Steegmuller's translation of Flaubert's letter to Louise Colet dated 11 August 1846.

> I did with you what I have done before with those I loved best: I showed them the bottom of the bag, and the acrid dust that rose from it made them choke. (FP 32)

> I did with you what *in the past* I have done with those I loved best: I *bared my soul*, and the acrid dust that rose from *its most secret recesses stuck in their throats.*[7]

The differences between Braithwaite's and Steegmuller's translations of the letters are slight but obvious, but do not suggest any significant effort to deny them validity as translations and nor does Braithwaite's version in any sense compromise the belief in the validity of the original archival source – the letter. Technical alterations in word choice do not challenge the validity of the archive in this instance. Similarly, when discussing the lives that Flaubert did not live, Braithwaite paraphrases Flaubert's own remarks about his mythical origins without any sense of the veracity of the archive being called into question. More pertinently, perhaps, there is not even the suggestion that Flaubert's remarks should be distrusted. Again there are technical alterations (feet to fathoms, the introduction of commas between the numbers, for example), but these differences serve to reinforce the recognizability between the two versions, to secure a stable context of interpretation.

Apart from the letters, Braithwaite also draws on other biographies in his effort to write his own. The fidelity demonstrated towards the letters is also evident in his references to these. His attack on Enid Starkie's contention that Flaubert mistook the colour of Emma Bovary's eyes is spitefully faithful to Starkie's *Flaubert: The Making of a Master*. This fidelity extends even as far as her footnotes.

It is not only those texts directly related to Flaubert that are presented as being a legitimate base for the biographical narrative but also those texts that provide the broader historical context. In particular, his references to G. M. Musgrave's *A Ramble through Normandy, or, Scenes, Characters and Incidents in a Sketching Excursion through Calvados* are precise (and, of course, referenced in order to allow the inquisitive reader the possibility of checking them). Musgrave's discussion of carriages suggests that the type used by Emma Bovary for her secret assignation in the Flaubert novel is much smaller than might have been imagined. This causes our view of the event to lurch 'suddenly' (*FP* 92). The archive is accepted as presenting a true account of the carriage that then necessitates a reconfiguration of our imagining of the scene. In other words, Braithwaite is working with a model of the archive that claims to provide direct access to the past.

Alison Lee suggests that Braithwaite's position with regard to the archive and his construction of Flaubert makes Braithwaite a 'Realist' character within a postmodern novel.[8] In other words, the acceptance of a stable archive does not produce a monolithic subject, but allows for the articulation of a subject that is complex and multiple. The idea of a static and pure identity being the inevitable result of a 'naive' conception of the validity of the archive is demonstrated as itself being naive. The textual presentation of Flaubert through the use of archival material produces a character that can be recognized as a unicity derived from the agglomeration of a set of (sometimes contradictory) subject positions.

The novel, too, is seeking a unicity derived from the heterogeneity of genres of discourse whose interrelationships produce mini-narratives within the total narrative of the quest. 'Pure Story', for example, like the two subsequent chapters, is both an epilogue and a conclusion. It is an epilogue to the discussion about Flaubert. The final three chapters provide us with more pieces of information about the writer, but, to all intents and purposes, the argument is over. 'Braithwaite's Dictionary of Accepted Ideas' ends his frantic collection and distribution of knowledge. It is as if he has now reached the point, after allowing the debate of 'The Case Against' and the alternative and scything views of his version of Louise Colet, that he can relax into a parody of the great man's last irony in his *Dictionnaire des idées reçues*. More than this, though, he can also allow a continuing and open-ended discussion about the man to continue without him. The final sentence of the final entry is, 'Discuss without concluding' (FP 159).

Having worked through his obsession with Flaubert, Braithwaite is now ready to tell the story for which Flaubert's has been the mask all along. 'Pure Story' is the account of Ellen's life and death, and of Braithwaite's responses to that life and death. The story aspect is important, as this chapter marks the climax of Braithwaite's narrative process.

In a final paradox, the opening of the door to the discovery of the parrot now that it need no longer be deferred diminishes the desire for the discovery at anything other than curiosity level. The final sentence of the book, which has Braithwaite apparently showing little interest even in this, has an interesting parallel earlier on in the novel. Having arrived at the discovery of three parrots in the Museum of Natural History, Braithwaite says, 'Perhaps it was one of them' (FP 190). On the one hand, this can be read as an acceptance of the impossibility of ever discovering the true parrot and effectively giving up on the idea, primarily because the more important truth about Ellen has been addressed. There is also the slightly less dispirited reading, which harks back to a similar use of the 'perhaps . . .' sentence, where the implication is that the 'perhaps' is in fact a statement of certainty in relation to Louise Colet knowing about a children's story: 'Perhaps Louise Colet knew it too' (FP 54).

This undecidability about the meaning of the last sentence is not surprising in a novel that has at practically every turn upset notions of narrative. It confuses the relationship between narrator and author; it subverts our expectations of narrative structure; it presents us with paradoxes, irreconcilable statements; it does not even answer the question it raises in the first chapter. But it does progress with an internal logic; it answers those questions that are particularly important to the narrator in a sequence that is consistent and regular; it enforces notions of the discrete ontological levels of the real and the fictional; it assumes the possibility of stable contexts of interpretation, but recognizes that this in itself does not assuage despair.

5

A Hundred Years of Solitude:
Staring at the Sun

The narrative structure of *Staring at the Sun* is similar to that of *Metroland*. There is a short, untitled opening section followed by three, numbered long sections. The three long sections chart the life of Jean Serjeant from her birth in 1922 to her final years in the 2020s. Each of these parts utilizes a discrete literary narrative form. The first part takes place during the late 1930s and extends to the early 1950s and could, therefore, be called a 'literary historical narrative'. The second takes place during the 1980s and is contemporaneous with the novel's writing and publication and could be called a 'literary narrative of the contemporary'. The final section is set in the near future (about the year 2010) and could be called a 'literary dystopian narrative'. There is not any determinable narrative form that links all of these separate narratives together. It is the lack of an operative literary meta-narrative in *Staring at the Sun* that led a great many reviewers to criticize the novel's supposed formlessness. Richard Ryner summed up many reviewers' frustrations by stating that the book reads like 'a novel in search of a structure', although Anthony Thwaite suggested that these concerns (which linked to whether the book was really a novel at all) were mundane and asked, 'do we need to be too much fussed by whether they are convincingly made "fictional" or not?'[1] Carlos Fuentes was unconcerned by the parochial nervousness about 'fiction', announcing that it was 'Brilliant ... Mr Barnes's work is at the forefront of a new internationalization of British fiction'.[2] Unsurprisingly, this quotation was used on the paperback edition from Picador.

It is the lack of a dominant narrative form within which the other narratives in the novel can be placed that shall be discussed first. The book begins with a description of Second World War fighter pilot Tommy Prosser's flight back from France, waiting to ambush German planes. It is 3.46 a.m. and Prosser sees the sun rise 'stately, inexorable, almost comic' (SS 1). Spying a ship apparently in distress, he descends very quickly, checks that the ship is safe, and then levels out at 8,000 feet: 'The speed of his descent had driven the sun back below the horizon, and as he looked towards the east he saw it rise again: the same sun coming up from the same place across the same sea . . . It was an ordinary miracle he would never forget' (SS 2). In this opening section many of the metaphors and motifs that are to appear throughout the novel are introduced. These metaphors and motifs are what provide the narrative with its power. Characters and story work as much through their relationships with these metaphors and motifs as they do in their own right. It is through this relationship that characters are linked to their previous selves, to each other, and to the story.

The dominating metaphors and motifs are introduced in this first section. The twice-seen sunrise instigates a structuring logic predicated on a binary order (sunrise–sunset, birth–death, faith–atheism). There is also the movement between the high and the low (plane–ship, air–sea, sky–land). There is the importance of the resonances and plays of colour, especially black and red; the presence of aeroplanes; the importance of sandwiches; and the jerking of necks.

Tonal comparisons are also set up with the bathetic description of the twice-seen sunrise being an 'ordinary miracle' (SS 2) being contrasted with the mystical effect it has on Prosser. The movement from the ridiculous to the sublime is mirrored in the structure of the book where the bathos of the opening section is weighed against the pathos of Jean's flight and twice-seen sunset on the final page.

The last of the important structuring features set up in the first section is the sliding between genres of discourse, the importance of which will be discussed presently. The story of Prosser's flight begins with a declarative statement ('This is what happened' (SS 1)). The opening of the first section proper

begins with an interrogative ('You ask me what life is?' (*SS* 3)).
This quotation is taken from a letter of Chekhov to Olga
Knipper, 20 April 1904: 'You ask me what life is? It is like
asking what a carrot is. A carrot is a carrot, and nothing more
is known' (*SS* 3). The book's two openings (the theme-image
opening of Prosser's descent, and the introduction to the story
of the life of Jean Serjeant) employ genres of discourse whose
modalities are discrete. The one's modality is certainty, the
other's anxiety.

The three long sections of the novel – the historical narrative,
the contemporary narrative, the science-fiction narrative – are
generically discrete. The effect and importance of discrete
genres of narration are spelled out in the text, in the first
paragraph:

> Sometimes the past was shot with a hand-held camera; sometimes
> it reared monumentally inside a proscenium arch with moulded
> plaster sways and floppy curtains; sometimes it eased along, a love
> story from the silent era, pleasing, out of focus and wholly
> implausible. And sometimes there was only a succession of stills
> to be borrowed from the memory. (*SS* 5)

This passage insists on a number of important things. First is
the way in which memory is a narrative event. Even when the
memory is called up in single images, they provide a 'suc-
cession'. There is, too, the recognition of a material and
historical constraint on the potential mode of the memory
narrated. The capacity to narrate within a particular discursive
framework (a silent movie, for example) requires that the
discursive framework is historically chronistic with the narrator. Also, the particular discursive framework that is employed bears a significance beyond the aesthetic, or rather the
aesthetic is implicated in a particular morality: 'The Incident
with Uncle Leslie – the very first Incident of her life – came in
a series of magic lantern slides. A sepia morality; the loveable
villain even had a moustache' (*SS* 5). Here a childhood
memory is narrated through an imagined aesthetic whose
discursive boundaries are created by the historical and biographical moment of the person being narrated. The magic
lantern slide works as sign of childhood (the biographical
moment of the narratee), and also as a sign of the early

twentieth century (the historical moment of the narrated). At a more general level, each of the literary narratives presents social narratives that are explored: marriage in section one; politics in section two; and the growth of information technology in section three.

The genre of discourse bears with it a morality (a nostalgic view of a time when the distinction between 'hero' and 'villain' was easy to make). This discrete discursive formulation exists within the dominating narrative discourse, which, in this section of the novel, is the narrative genre of the historical novel. Later the narrative genres alter, yet the character (Leslie) and the motifs that circulate around and through him (hyacinths, golf tees, 'the old green heaven', and so on) still persist. The novel, then, performs as well as presents its themes: uncertainty and change fighting against security and knowledge

In the first section of the novel, as with Chris in *Metroland*, Jean is ever-questioning. Everything seems important to her, yet everything is unfathomable. This, in turn, leads to a sense of guilt: 'Even so, Jean felt obscurely that her inability to understand the European crisis was partly responsible for its continuation' (*SS* 18). Her presumed ignorance and continuing guilt appear to find a solution in the form of Michael, who is a policeman and seems to know things, to be responsible, and whom Jean imagines she loves. She and Michael marry and Jean is fulfilled: 'Michael was the answer, whatever might have been the question' (*SS* 36). The degree to which Jean's seeming inability to understand anything as a young woman has led a number of reviewers to argue that she lacks credibility. David Crossen spoke for many when he called her 'impossibly naive', and even a sympathetic critic such as Allan Massie suggested that 'Jean is almost a simpleton'.[3]

Her marriage, though, is far from being an answer. Before the disappointment of marriage, Jean had looked on it as an ending ('Getting married was an end, not a beginning. Why else did so many films and books finish at the altar?' (*SS* 62)), and this feeling of ending, of closure, has the cast of an answer for Jean. At the end of the first section she 'felt now that she knew all the secrets; all the secrets of her life' (*SS* 63).

The secrets, though, as she soon discovers from her husband, Michael, are that she is 'abysmally stupid, barren, unnatural'

(*SS* 70); that 'woman' can be 'beaten and sharpened until it ha(s) an edge for slashing with' (*SS* 71); that Marie Stopes's book has no more use than 'faded graffiti briefly glimpsed on the wall of a country bus shelter' (*SS* 72); that 'you could be intelligent with one person and stupid with another' (*SS* 70). She also learns that, far from being the promised 'first-rate life', marriage has given her a 'second-rate life' (*SS* 74). Marriage as an answer, as a social narrative, as a closed genre of discourse, is seen to be stultifying, degenerative, and dangerous for the individual who prioritizes it.

The physical and verbal violence suffered by Jean, her boredom, and the epigraph 'Three wise men – are you serious? – graffito c.1984' (*SS* 65) set up the dominant social narrative of the second section of the novel. In this section Jean leaves Michael, gives birth to her son, Gregory, travels the world, and runs into Rachel, 'the least probable of all Gregory's girl-friends' (*SS* 112).

The character of Rachel is, compared to the other characters in the novel, loud and strident. As a character she dominates the section, as the genre of discourse of which she is a part (polemical politics) seeks to dominate their genres. She is constructed as a believer of postcard politics, the world of throwaway insults and absolute conviction. One of her phrases ('*Three* wise men – are you serious?') is also the epigraph to the section, and is followed up with a series of bold assertions and rhetorical questions unsupported by any sense of argument:

> Rachel said: 'If they can put one man on the moon, why don't they put them all there?' Rachel said: 'A woman needs a man like a tree needs a dog with a lifted leg.' ... Rachel said: 'A man on a white charger is all very well, but who's going to clear up the droppings?' Rachel said: 'Being born a woman is being born left-handed and forced to write with the other one. No wonder we stammer.' Rachel said: 'You think I'm shouting? You don't know how deaf they are.' (*SS* 123–4)

The way in which the propositions are simply listed has the effect of making Rachel appear clamorous and unconvincing. This could suggest that the novel is antipathetic to feminism (or a particular version of it), but the character of Jean might be seen to contradict this view. In the terms of the present argument, it is not the specific political discourse that is employed by Rachel that is being scrutinized but the type of discourse of which it is representative. Her life is the lived expression of a particular genre of discourse, this genre being summed up in her exasperated plea to Jean that: 'You just have to be normal [to be a feminist]. You just have to see things as they are' (SS 124). This assumes that a political discourse that is prescriptive (it tells people what to do in order to achieve a particular state of affairs) can be derived from a discourse that is descriptive (that tells people how things are). The descriptive is itself a fraught area because it assumes a shared response to a particular stimulus. To claim, as Rachel does, that a political discourse (a project predicated on a set of prescriptives) can be validated by or derived from a description of a set of social phenomena is both methodologically unsound and unjust. This is because one is translating phrases from one genre of discourse (description) into another one (prescription).

The belief of Rachel that her description of the world is correct and that, from this, she can provide an explanation and a programme of change not only threatens violence to other discourses, but also threatens the identity of the individual who exists solely within it. She sets herself up, and the world, as mono-discursive, and, in the same way as Braithwaite's lonely-hearts advertisement, this reduces the possibility of a full and varied expression of self. Jean is aware of this danger but still yearns for the knowledge that 'she would carry on being herself' (SS 25). There is a bravery, for Jean, in believing at the end of your life what you believed at the beginning (SS 181) but this is tempered in the novel with the demonstration of the totalitarian implications of this. This is particularly evident with Rachel's assurance about her own position: 'Rachel not only knew her own mind, she knew other people's as well, especially Gregory's' (SS 112).

The final genre of discourse, which promises closure and knowledge, is the Total Absolute Truth machine, whose acronymical pun 'TAT' is self-explanatory. Its little brother is the General Purpose Computer, on which the accumulated knowledge of the world is stored. This computer can provide information about everything, but it will provide opinions or speculation about nothing. Questions must simply demand facts, they must assume the world as an object of cognition. To enter into a speculative discourse is to disobey the system; in fact, it is to be denied by the system. A speculative interrogative is met with the response 'NOT REAL QUESTION' (SS 175). In the name of the democratization of knowledge, the pursuit of knowledge has been forsaken. By placing these social narratives that promise closure within a heterogeneous play of genres that discourage closure, the novel seems to tend towards a 'postmodern' notion of a knowledge that prioritizes heterogeneity, dissensus, and openness.[4]

It is left to the characters themselves to divine a meaning, and that meaning necessitates a pattern to their lives, a narrative. For Jean this comes to pointing out 'the things in your life which were different from the things in theirs' (SS 182). She pretends a certainty in order to relieve Gregory of the pain of searching. He asks, 'Is death absolute?'

> 'Yes, dear.' The reply was firm and exact, declining the need for supplementary questions.
> 'Is religion nonsense?'
> 'Yes, dear.'
> 'Is suicide permissible?'
> 'No, dear.'   (SS 185)

Even this poignant certainty is recognized as being unsteady: 'Old age had its arrogance, after all' (SS 186). Jean's aim is for a narrative logic: 'she just wanted it [a film] to turn out properly, correctly, in accordance with its own logic. It was like this with the film of your life' (SS 125). Gregory, however, does not believe in the possibility of answers, of closure: 'It wasn't like that, Gregory thought. First you had the questions and sought the answers. Then you had answers and wondered what the questions were. Finally, you realized that the question and the answer were the same, the one enclosed the other' (SS 189). All that Gregory requires is a pattern. In a discussion of jazz, Gregory's ideas are made explicit. He divides jazz into three periods and decides that the second period, the one 'when they played scraps of tunes, brief, repeated phrases, shy melodies no sooner begun than aborted', chimes most with his outlook (SS 183).

Yet, Gregory is looking for more certainty than this. He requires belief, faith. He writes a list of possible permutations about the existence of God. Ultimately he simply believes 'because it was true; it was true because he knew it was true. As for what was true, or what followed from what was true, he couldn't be so presumptuous. . . . You didn't deny God if he turned out to be unjust. Who ever thought God had to be just? God only had to be true' (SS 188–9). For Gregory, truth is not a necessary condition of justice. In fact, truth and justice are discrete, judgement is not validated through an appeal to truth (a prescriptive is not derived from a descriptive). Giving answers, making judgements, both of these acts are rendered doubtful in the novel. Neither Jean nor Gregory is willing to advise or pronounce with any certainty. Even when they do, their certainty is undercut or made self-conscious. Without this certainty, lives are made difficult to know and even harder to judge. The opening sentence of the third section is 'How do you tell a good life from a bad life, a wasted life?' (SS 139). This question remains unanswered, although heavily pondered. The same is true of most of the questions in the novel, and, importantly, none of the questions is deemed to have any greater significance than any other.

Neither questions nor genres of discourse are seen to be of any greater significance than any other. The equivalence of genre, discourse, narrative, and the rest results, in this formulation, in the depthless or affectless state of the postmodern. In Staring at the Sun, it is possible to see the equivalence of genre, the equivalence of all types of question, and the inconclusiveness of questioning itself as a demonstration of this depthlessness.

Staring at the Sun investigates the possibility of knowledge, particularly as it is articulated through different narrative forms. It insists upon the necessity of paying attention to the form of knowledge (how it is transmitted, by whom, for what purpose and with what grounding) as much as to what the particular knowledge might be. It is also very concerned to probe the ways in which this knowledge might be used to justify and legitimate different ethical positions, whether they be the permissibility of suicide, the existence of God, the judgement of character, the nature of love, or the accumulation and dissemination of knowledge itself.

6

Fables, not the Reconstruction:
A History of the World in 10½ Chapters

A History of the World in 10½ Chapters was published in 1989.
It was greeted by many reviewers with a muted enthusiasm.
The formal ingenuity of the novel was highly praised, but the
capacity of the author to sustain the weight of the novel under
such formal pressure was put into question. The extent to
which the novel's form might be considered a reason for its
eventual failure to achieve its possibilities will be discussed
later in the chapter in relation to its own examination of art's
potential to act as a barrier against the effects of history.

The four novels preceding this one, for all their formal
ingenuity and inventiveness, have remained within at least one
recognizable feature of novelistic discourse: they have all had
a narrator or main character who provides a narrative cohe-
sion. *A History of the World in 10½ Chapters* dispenses with
character to the extent that there are entirely new persons in
each chapter, and it dispenses with story to the extent that each
new chapter has a new location and time with no necessary or
obvious link to the previous or subsequent chapter. A brief
synopsis should serve to make this clear.

Chapter 1, 'The Stowaway', is narrated by a woodworm
seemingly in the present, although it claims to have been
aboard Noah's Ark. The exact location of the story is obviously
difficult to discern, but it starts in Armenia and finishes at
Mount Ararat. Chapter 2, 'The Visitors', is a third-person
account of the hijacking of the *Santa Euphemia* sometime in the

41

1980s and takes in destinations from Venice to the Cyclades. The third chapter, 'The Wars of Religion', is set in a small village in France in the sixteenth century and is comprised of official documents relating to the trial of termites. 'The Survivor', the fourth chapter, seems to be a little way in the future, in Australia, and is a first- and third-person account of a supposed nuclear disaster. 'Shipwreck' is divided into two sections. The first is a description of the events that led up to the wrecking of *The Medusa* in West Africa in the early nineteenth century. The second is an analysis and brief history of the Gericault painting of the same event. 'The Mountain' is set at a similar time but involves an expedition to Mount Ararat in order to find the remains of Noah's Ark. 'Three Simple Stories' lives up to its name and gives us three stories that range from 1960s English suburbia to Nineveh to the Falkland Islands, to Germany, to Cuba, to the USA; from biblical times to the late nineteenth century to the mid-twentieth century. 'Upstream' takes us to the jungle via a series of letters written by a film actor. 'Parenthesis' is apparently narrated by Barnes himself[1] from the comfort of his own bed and a friend's kitchen. 'Project Ararat' transports us back to Ararat in the company of an American astronaut in the mid-1970s. And 'The Dream' takes place in someone's head but represents Heaven.

A distinction needs to be made between the way that historical events are presented in various chapters, and the theorization of historical recording that is given in 'Parenthesis'. The easy elision between theory and practice that so many of the reviewers of the book discussed is not so obvious as they suggested. This, however, is not necessarily a weakness of the novel, as I shall argue when discussing its ideas of art.

The most explicit account of historical recording and the nature of history is given in 'Parenthesis'. The positioning of this half-chapter is important as whatever theory is given comes, in some respects, after the fact. By the time the reader gets to 'Parenthesis', he or she will already have read eight chapters. These chapters will all have been recounting different stories from different periods, but the reader will also have noticed the strange overlaps of motifs and images, will have been aware of analogous points of contact between chapters.

When, therefore, the novel provides its theory of history as 'fabulation', there is a twofold sense of recognition. First the reader is aware that this is what the novel has been doing and so proves the theory; and, secondly, he or she will have been aware that this is what he or she, as a reader, has been recognizing, and so again the theory is proven. This is the novel's theory of fabulation:

> And while we fret and writhe in bandaged uncertainty – are we a voluntary patient? – we fabulate. We make up a story to cover the facts we don't know or can't accept; we keep a few true facts and spin a new story round them. Our panic and our pain are only eased by soothing fabulation; we call it history. (*HW* 242)

History, then, is fabulation, and fabulation is the way in which we make sense of our present situation by inventing narratives of our past. Fabulation is an overcoming of chaos, a necessary and soothing practice that provides coherence and stability amid an otherwise daunting array of disparate and unassimilable facts. In this formulation the novel's use of the term is closely allied to its dictionary sense, which is 'To relate as a fable or a myth. To talk or narrate in fables'. This definition raises a number of difficulties. It would seem to suggest that history is not the devastating and malevolent force implied elsewhere in the book, but, rather, a cosy bedtime story. This definition is one that Barnes seemed to be working with when he was interviewed by Kate Saunders. He says:

> I thought, what can we put up against the 24 wheeler that's bearing down on us all the time called history, with its little truck at the back called politics? The three main answers are religion, art and love. I think that religion isn't true, and art doesn't work for everyone. Love is the final fall-back position.[2]

It would also suggest that history, as a fable or myth, is simply a fiction.

An analysis of the other chapters will show how this is far from the idea of history that Barnes has been providing his readers with. Even within 'Parenthesis', however, this idea does not stand up. Importantly, the idea of salvation that fabulation seems to demand by easing our panic and our pain is explicitly rejected by the text: 'Our love has gone, and it is the fault of the history of the world' (*HW* 246). Here salvation is denied, hope is banished, and it is history that is blamed. This is much more in line with what would appear to be the novel's thesis in the other chapters. The contradiction between the two uses of the term 'history' seems to me to stem from an attitude to narrative. What is brutal, frightening, and degrading about the history of the world is not the stories that link events together (this is 'soothing' fabulation), but the events themselves, those moments in time, moments in space, where human ignorance, stupidity, violence, and hate are laid bare. These moments, which can last for a minute or for years, which can cover the planet or take place on the bridge of a ship, astonish and appal us and can be made bearable only through narrative. This places narrative in a double-bind, however, as these moments are themselves articulated only through narrative.

What *A History of the World in 10½ Chapters* does is to place a series of mini-narratives, relating to moments, into a fabulatory structure. The structure is fabulatory in two, apparently contradictory, ways. The first way that it is fabulatory is that it mimics, in attenuated form, the pattern of biblical narrative – a narrative whose ultimate purpose is to soothe and provide salvation. The first chapter pays a very obvious debt to the flood story from Genesis', and the last chapter, 'The Dream', less obviously, draws from Revelations. (It is interesting how prominent the flood story and Genesis were during the 1980s as a means for expressing a feminist or ecological politics. Among some of the novels that used this pre-text are *Boating for Beginners* by Jeanette Winterson (1985), *Not Wanted on the Voyage* by Timothy Findley (1985), and Steven Minot's *Surviving the Flood* (1983).) The second method of structural fabulation is the way in which the novel itself creates impertinent links and strange connections between chapters, forcing the implication of causality and meaning. Again, then, we are faced with a contradiction. The moments of horror are presented in a narrative that, presumably, is intended to demonstrate the inevitable folly of humanity and are simultaneously recuperated within a twin fabulatory structure whose purpose is to soothe the effects of these moments.

The history of the world that the novel offers is kaleidoscopic, seemingly unconnected – a collection of disparate events and times with little causal connection between one story and its predecessor. This apparent chaos of history, though, is formally bounded within the rigidly teleological structure Genesis to Revelations. The tension between absolute historical narrative and fragmentary ones is here manifest in the form of the novel. That the novel's readers may well not believe in either the flood or the idea of heaven is not important. What is important is that the teleology that the Bible demonstrates functions for the novel as a metaphor for both what is desired and for what is impossible to achieve – the certainty that fabulation can provide.

Any stable notion of what history is in the novel is difficult to grasp. What is certain, however, is that it is very worried by it. It is worried by the brutality of specific events and by the way these events are sanitized through narrative. According to the narrator of 'Parenthesis', there are, or have been, three main ways in which this worry has been assuaged: religion, art, and love.

This assertion carries with it some difficulties. It would appear that the part of history that these things are supposed to be resisting is its chaotic and brutalizing aspect. The novel's own thesis seems to imply that this is achieved perfectly adequately by the act of narrativization, of fabulation. At this point it is necessary to see each chapter as a part of the whole thesis. A chapter such as 'The Visitors' stands here as an example of the dangers of the fabulatory exercise in so far as it demonstrates the potential for conflict between competing fabulations.

Franklin Hughes is a television personality whose programmes have been about history. He is giving a series of lectures on a cruise ship. He has taken Tricia along as his assistant and it is said that she is this year's fling, that he is mildly in love with her. During the course of one of his lectures he is interrupted by the arrival of Arab terrorists, the visitors of the title.

The hijacking of the *Santa Euphemia* of the story bears a close resemblance to the hijacking of the *Achille Lauro* in 1985. This is particularly the case in the division of the passengers into nationalities, a division that will affect which of the passengers is killed first should the terrorists' demands not be met. A

45

division made first by God and then by Noah if the wood-worm-narrator of the first story 'The Stowaway' is to believed. Franklin Hughes has an Irish passport and is therefore one of the nationalities least likely to be shot. His girlfriend of the moment, Tricia, has a British passport and, therefore, is a likely candidate to die early. Hughes, whose Irish passport makes him innocent of the colonial crimes of the British, tries to convince the visitors that Tricia is his wife, therefore Irish by marriage, therefore innocent by default, therefore last in line to get shot. He will be allowed Tricia's innocence only if he gives a lecture stating the aims and historical circumstances of the hijackers. His choice is between an act of altruism that will be seen as self-interested cowardice (saving Tricia's life by doing the bidding of the Arabs) or a selfishness that will be seen as nobility (keeping true to his principles while condemning Tricia to death).

Hughes's status as a well-known historian invests him with an authority that allows his histories, his fabulations, to have validity, to have a higher value than the passengers'. But this status is provisional and contingent. The history he is compelled to tell of the recent developments in the Middle East is not the soothing fabulation of the Euro-American tradition but the disruptive fabulation, to that tradition, of the Arab nations. Hughes is telling the wrong story. The hostility towards him from the passengers is due partly to his perceived cowardice, but also to a more fundamental fear that historical records are not inviolable; that one person's fable is another person's instrument of terror.

If both the moments of history and their threading into a narrative are seen as dangerous, how might religion, art, and love be said to help, to stand up to history? They are being set up in contrast to history, outside history, transcendentally. The assumption is that religion functions for the individual believer in an ahistorical way. The cause for a particular prayer or ceremony might be an event in the lived experience of that individual (might, therefore, be a part of history), but the act and object of devotion are outside the strict contingencies bearing on that person.

The novel's problem with religion, though, is not its meta-physical aspect but the fact that it is 'either wimpishly workaday, or terminally crazy, or merely businesslike confusing spirituality with charitable donations' (*HW* 244). In other words, it is too much a part of the world, too limp or too fundamental to be of any good to people wanting relief. Much of *A History of the World in 10½ Chapters* has been devoted to proving this thesis. Noah and God are both seen as tyrannical and selfish. The early modern Christian church is painted as ridiculous and unscrupulous. Nineteenth-century evangelism is seen as callous and unforgiving. Twentieth-century evangelism is seen as bigoted and foolish. Missionaries are portrayed as proud and ultimately futile. Religion and terrorism are seen as inextricably entwined. And, finally, in 'The Dream', Heaven is represented as an illusion, as a rather weak and obvious product of wish-fulfilment that can sustain itself as an idea only for as long as the individual can invent things worth wishing for. In a consumerist world of instant gratification and mundane motivation, this vision of Heaven is little more than a depressingly conventional decadence. In this way religion fails as much because people have lost the imaginative capacity to reinvent it usefully as because of its own shortcomings.

The novel's dismissal of religion is necessary in order for it to be able to work through art and love as possible replacements, but the religion it discusses is predominantly Western and seems to show no recognition of the continuing (indeed growing) amount of religious activity around the world. The picture painted would seem to make religion a non-option in the struggle against history, but the reader must ask him or herself how far the novel's history of religion is itself simply fabulation.

The contradictions relating to the novel's conception of history and the blatant bias of its representation of religion have the effect of destabilizing the reader's faith in the novel as a whole. In a sense this is an invalid criticism in that the novel is precisely that, a novel. The fact that it broaches ideas and does not make them cohere completely might be a fault in a book of philosophy, but in a novel as heterogeneous as this one it is almost a recommendation. If, however, this non-coherence is to be seen as a fault and the book is to be considered in some senses a failure, then this has been written into it from the start.

The first chapter is a demonstration of the failure of religion to provide sense and resistance. The subsequent three stories show the failure of various systems and by the time we reach 'Shipwreck' art is about ready to receive its due.

As with religion, art as a concept to put up *against* history is seen as being *outside* history. Art is the expression of humanity's resilience, of its transcendence. Art helps us to stand outside history and, in so doing, to understand it better, and also, perhaps, to forgive it:

> We have to understand it, of course, this catastrophe; to understand it, we have to imagine it so we need the imaginative arts. But we also need to justify it and forgive it, this catastrophe, however minimally. Why did it happen, this mad act of Nature, this crazed human moment? Well, at least it produced art. Perhaps, in the end, that's what catastrophe is *for*. (*HW* 125)

Such a bold claim for the redemptive powers of art is troubling. John Naughton, reviewing a televison interview between Barnes and Melvyn Bragg, wondered why Barnes had been unable to explain the phrase 'that's what catastrophe is *for*' and was similarly concerned that Bragg had allowed him to get away the 'old baloney' that Barnes offered as an argument.[3] The boldness of the statement seems to invite scrutiny and even hostility. However, it is necessary to read it as part of the novel as a whole and not as an isolated comment. Trying to find some reason for those violent moments of history has been part of the novel's purpose. It is to maintain some hope for the possibility of discerning a reason to history that art is championed in such a way.

Unfortunately, and unsurprisingly, there are difficulties with this. The first is a practical one. 'People die; rafts rot; and works of art are not exempt' (*HW* 139). Works of art are just as prone to time's relentlessness as anything else, and this hinders their transcendental, redemptive powers. Another, more immediate and pertinent concern is that, even taking into account art's relative longevity when compared to a human life, art's potential for redemption 'isn't accessible to all, or where accessible isn't always inspiring or welcome' (*HW* 245). One need only read some of the reviews of *A History of the World in 10½ Chapters* to see this assertion illustrated.

The novel itself as a proof of its own thesis of art's failure, or at least inability, to provide a defence against history is worth noting. It takes catastrophes and turns them into art, and moreover an art that is committed to the idea of art. Its commitment lies in its attempt to find a genuine combat to history while recognizing the inevitable failure of its own enterprise as a work of art. It draws attention to the inconsistencies of its own argument and structure and is in a permanent state of collapse. It necessitates its own deconstruction, but at the same time demands that this deconstruction does not deny the claims that it is putting forward. The tension between the textual strategies being deployed that are predicated on notions of the relativity of truth and the deferral of meaning, and the demand for notions of truth in the body of the text, means that these faults are obvious. As a text, a piece of art, it is pointing to itself and saying that it is not enough.

What is enough is love. Love, according to the narrator of 'Parenthesis', is 'the final fall-back position' after religion and art have failed. Like religion and art, its strength lies in its capacity to work outside the narrative framework insisted upon by history and fabulation. The very fact that the novel's essay on love is called 'Parenthesis' (that it is 'an explanatory or qualifying word, clause or sentence inserted into a passage with which it has not necessarily any grammatical connexion' or 'a passage introduced into a context with which it has no connexion; a digression') demonstrates this thematic idea structurally.

In relation to the novel's ideas on history, the chapter is both explanatory and qualifying but far from being conclusive. With respect to love, though, an explanatory focus is a little harder to find, although its qualifying impulse is totally unambiguous – that without love the history of the world is obscene. A number of quotations powerfully confirm this:

> The history of the world becomes brutally self-important without love. (*HW* 240)
>
> [Love will] teach us to stand up to history. (*HW* 240)
>
> How you cuddle in the dark governs how you see the history of the world. (*HW* 241)
>
> Love is anti-mechanical, anti-materialist that's why bad love is still good love. (*HW* 244)

And I'm not saying that love will make you happy . . . But you can believe this and still insist that love is our only hope. (*HW* 245)

We must believe in it or we're lost . . . If we don't then we merely submit to the history of the world and to somebody else's truth. (*HW* 246)

The chapter offers us anecdotes, ideas, and aphorisms about love, but does not tell us what love is – only what it is not and what it does. Apart from the sense of love affirming something – essentially the capacity to survive – there is the marvellously polyglot discussion of the words 'I love you'. 'Parenthesis' places the importance of love in its relationship to truth. The novel's angry cry is that if, one day, we lose our capacity for love then 'it is the fault of the history of the world' (*HW* 246). Its hope is that there is a connection between and a salvation in the union of love and truth: 'Love and truth, that's the vital connection, love and truth' (*HW* 240). This hope is little more than that, and is predicated on a faith that has suffered horribly at the hands of the novel thus far. All we can do is believe that 'objective truth is obtainable; or . . . that it is 99 per cent obtainable; or if we can't believe this, we must believe that 43 per cent objective truth is better than 41 per cent. We must do so, because if we don't we're lost, we fall into beguiling relativity . . .' (*HW* 246).

An amorphous concept that will fail but that still offers salvation: this is the novel's preferred redemption. Franklin Hughes aboard the *Santa Euphemia* can be seen as an illustration of these terms. In 'The Visitors' Franklin Hughes is asked to occupy two incompatible positions in relation to the story he is told to tell. The possibility of his selfless act of love for Tricia being recognized is absolutely denied by the structural conditions of the telling of the story and the way this positions him as its teller. An act of loving selflessness is seen as an act of gross selfishness and cowardice. Love has positively hurt Hughes, and yet it did give him the courage, for an instant, to stand up to History. The seeming failure of love to guarantee happiness (as in the case of Franklin Hughes) or even to produce happiness on its own terms is accounted for in the novel like this:

And I'm not saying that love will make you happy – above all, I'm not saying that. If anything, I tend to think that it will make you unhappy: either immediately unhappy, as you are impaled by incompatibility, or unhappy later, when the woodworm has been quietly gnawing for years and the bishop's throne collapses. But you can believe this and still insist that love is our only hope. (*HW* 245)

That love is hope even if it fails is demonstrated in the stories in the novel. Only three of the tales have obvious descriptions of loving relationships, and of these only one presents a vaguely optimistic illustration of its possibilities.

Kath Ferris in 'The Survivor' is driven to escape/breakdown by the disintegration of her relationship with her partner, Greg. Whether she is dying from radioactive fallout or suffering psychotic delusions in a hospital, her situation appears bleak. However, Kath has retained the belief in and the capacity to feel and express love. The cats that she takes with her on her voyage have seemingly been practising their own version of amatory relationship, and Linda, the female cat, ends the story by giving birth to a litter of kittens. Kath's response to this is immediate and absolute: 'She felt such love. The cat wouldn't let her touch the kittens, of course, but that was all right, that was normal. She felt such happiness! Such hope!'(*HW* 111). Whether in delirium or dying, Kath's capacity to survive (and she is the only character explicitly called a survivor in the book) is related directly to her capacity to love. And the fact that the cats are called Paul and Linda makes the entire little group, perhaps, a band on the run.

The other lovers in the book do not fare as well. Franklin Hughes's decision to give the lecture in order to guarantee the safety of Tricia leads, in fact, to her never speaking to him again. The point is not, though, that love failed but that, in a moment of extreme historical contingency, Hughes 'stood up to history', ignored its 'chin-out strut', and said 'by the way what a silly uniform you're wearing' (*HW* 240). The lover, in a moment of selflessness, attempted to transcend the historical moment.

Charlie's letters in 'Upstream' demonstrate a movement from narcissist to lover, and not just the lover of a specific object but of humanity. He writes what amounts to a confessional to his wife, Pippa, and, in one of his final letters after the death of his co-actor, Matt, and just before he leaves the

51

jungle for Caracas, he illustrates his new-found subjectivity. He says that in Caracas he is going to find any copy of the *Daily Telegraph* and read all the bits he normally just skirts over, like the nature section and the cricket scores. Also he says:

> Maybe I'll read the births column as well. To Emma and Nicholas, a daughter, Suzie, sister to Alexander and Bill. Good old Alexander and Bill, I'll say, now you've got little Suzie to play with. You must be gentle with her, you must protect her all your lives, she's your little sister, you must make her the apple of your eye. God I'm crying Pippa, the tears are just streaming down my face. (*HW* 214)

While Charlie might appear a little sentimental, he has, despite his earlier boorishness, attempted at some sort of imaginative engagement with an other as a subject. Charlie, when faced with the contingencies of history, has found no relief in either religion or art. Art, represented by the film that he is acting in, has been the cause of his pain and, having caused it, is unable to provide any relief from its effects. Religion, in the guise of the priestly simulacra he has been enacting, has also proven itself unresponsive to the needs of Charlie, but, more importantly, its part in the creation of historical narratives, in its attempted imposition of a single story, has been shown to have tragic consequences for whole cultures as well as for individuals. The film, and the story it is presenting, are also both indicative of the West's colonization of other areas of the world, first through religion, then multinational capitalism (signified by the Coca-Cola signs near the jungle), and now by the spread of high-tech information systems. Charlie has had to accept love as the final fallback position. His love for Pippa has enabled him to cope with, stand up to, history. 'Love won't change the history of the world,' says the narrator in 'Parenthesis', 'but it will teach us to stand up to it' (*HW* 240). Charlie's love for Pippa could not stop the death of Matt but it can help him cope.

Unfortunately for Charlie, contingencies have reared their ugly heads. Love fails drastically, but it is the reader's recognition of what that failure means, the return to selfishness, to arrogance, to self-pity and narcissism, that proves the novel's point. And also, for a time, the belief in love had enabled Charlie to resist the torments of history.

A History of the World in 10½ Chapters is in many respects a bleak novel. History is seen to be either a malevolent force that curtails and threatens human potentiality, or a set of narratives that are both resistant to verification and responsible for ignorance and atrocities. There is nothing to legitimate these narratives except an appeal to faith, and faith itself is seen as either redundant or damaging. Efforts to locate legitimation outside the narrative framework are either specious (as in the case of religion and art) or liable to failure (like love). It is to love, and its potential to act as a redeeming force, that Barnes turns in the next novel, *Talking It Over*.

7

You Talking to Me? *Talking It Over*

Talking It Over is the story of Oliver and Stuart, best friends from school, and Gillian. The stolid, unglamorous Stuart has met Gillian and fallen in love with her. The three characters spend a lot of time together until Stuart and Gillian marry, at which point the flamboyant, erudite Oliver falls calamitously in love with Gillian too. The movement of Gillian from Stuart to Oliver, and the effect this has on the characters' relationships with each other, and the reversals effected on their lives, is the main thrust of the story. The method of representing this story is the point of departure for this chapter.

There are nine assigned first-person narrators in *Talking It Over*, as well as one medical document independently labelled. The three main narrators are Stuart, Oliver, and Gillian, and it is through these that the bulk of the story is told. The story, simple as it seems, is told through the complementary and contradictory monologues of the nine narrators. This formal device allows for varying versions of the same set of events to be read by the reader, leaving it up to him or her to decide which of the differing accounts he or she is going to trust. The apparently small-scale love story allied with the narrative technique did not win universal approval. D. J. Taylor called it a 'Hampstead novel decked out in pretty camouflage', while James Buchan noted the unflattering similarity to Martin Amis's *Success*, commenting that Barnes was lucky to have escaped 'Amisville . . . with his fancy French threads in tatters, a broken finger on his writing hand and a gash in his reputation which will need stitches'.[1]

Both the story itself and the narrative strategies employed to represent it foreground the problems of judgement and veracity, with particular emphasis in the story on their relationship to love and truth. Quite who the characters are talking to is never resolved, but it is through him or her that their stories reach the reader. Often the reader knows more than the characters, which implies a certain secrecy between the characters that it is part of the novel to unravel. One of these secrets and its subsequent discovery by Oliver (Stuart's and Gill's method of meeting) is the catalyst for the drama of the tale. Stuart's sense of betrayal at Oliver's discovery, and Oliver's eventual marrying of Gill, are the main movements of the story. Oliver's justification to the reader for what Stuart sees as betrayal is this:

> Put yourself in my *pantoufles*. Would you renounce your love, slip gracefully from the scene, become a goatherd and play mournfully consoling music on your Panpipes all day while your heedless flock chomp the succulent tufts? People don't *do* that. People never did. Listen, if you go off and become a goatherd you never loved her in the first place. Or you loved the melodramatic gesture more. Or the goats. Perhaps pretending to fall in love was merely a smart career move allowing you to diversify into pasturing. But you didn't *love* her. (*TIO* 80)

Oliver's career-minded goatherd demonstrates that, for Oliver, love is above the economic. This becomes an important aspect of the novel's discussion of love as it progresses.

In *Talking It Over* the possibility of love is investigated in two ways. The first is a direct confrontation between love and the discourses that support it, and the market and the discourses that support that. The second is the way in which the love for a person is affected by the contexts in which that person is recognized and understood.

The confrontation between 'love' and 'the market' is not as simplistic as it might seem. In the first instance there is nothing to suggest that simply because Stuart works in a bank he is somehow incapable of loving; there is no direct structural relationship between the occupation and the mentality. His response to Gill's loving him might appear sentimental, but it is certainly not infused with a market discourse:

I hugged her. I put my arms around her and hugged her, but I
didn't kiss her again because I thought I might cry. Then I hugged
her again and pushed her through the door because I thought that
if it lasted any longer I *would* cry. I stood on the doorstep alone,
pressing my lids together, breathing in, breathing out. (*TIO* 36)

Stuart's conception of love is a strongly individualistic one,
however. He does not, at this point, see love in terms of
economics as a system of exchange values, but he does regard
it as something that can be *acquired* through sensible speculation. By paying £25 to go to a singles' party, you might be able
to find love. In other words, the process of being in love evades
the systems of the market, but in order to be able to be a part
of that process market decisions need to be made. Oliver
makes this point as a way of castigating Stuart, but fails to
recognize two related implications. He says:

> Apparently there are these locations for the amatoriously parched
> to which they can repair four times on successive Fridays, all for
> the sum of £25. I was shocked – that was my first reaction. Then I
> thought, well, don't ever underestimate furry little Stu. Trust him
> to go about the business of L'Amour like a market re-
> searcher. (*TIO* 146)

Apart from the refusal to engage with the fact that Gill was
also there and therefore also a 'market researcher', Oliver
avoids the more fundamental problem (as had Stuart) relating
to the social contexts in which love might be possible. Gill pays
attention to this social involvement when she considers her
first month of marriage to Stuart. She describes her brief time
as a social worker and then relates what she remembers about
that to her potential future with Stuart, especially her desire
that, unlike her clients, Stuart does not get disappointed. The
dramatic irony that this passage accrues as the novel progresses is worth taking note of here, as it has direct relevance to
the relationship between the discourses of love and the market.
Stuart does get disappointed and this disappointment causes
him to reject the discourse of love in favour of that of the
market. His disappointment, though, is itself represented in
market terms by Oliver.

Oliver, before Stuart is sure about his affair with Gill, goes
round to Stuart's one night expecting the three of them to go

to the cinema. Soon after his arrival, he hands Stuart an envelope of money that he owes Stuart from a previous loan. This is an explicit clearing of debts before he feels he is able to take his wife off him. And it is with precisely this sort of language that Oliver is working. This is partly because he feels that it is a language that Stuart will understand, and partly because it is a 'riff' that he is enjoying. It is also, though, because he does at some level regard Gill as the property of Stuart, and as such he needs to buy her. She is an object, and Stuart and Oliver have to try and arrange some exchange value that will allow the transfer of ownership, 'What would he take for her now? What's his mark up?' (TIO 147).

Both Stuart and Oliver succumb to the temptation of talking about love as though it were simply a part of an economy, of the market, and are speaking in a form of inert language, unable or unwilling to find an idiom outside the dominant discourse with which to search for an expression. The totalitarianism of late capitalism is precisely the inability to think outside its discourses, to find a new idiom that is not immediately neutralized by appropriation into the dominant discourse. To paraphrase Jean-François Lyotard from his essay 'A Gloss on Resistance', when the desire to try and find the possibility of saying something that you do not know how to say is lost, when language is thought to be unable to exceed its own limits, then you have a version of Newspeak. When the language of love becomes itself subject to the law of Newspeak, then the possibility of resisting the domination of the market is given up.

Stuart, after the betrayal of Oliver and Gillian, sinks himself into the market. This is partly a pragmatic gesture. He works in a bank and that work provides security and coherence. It has the added advantage of being a system that, however complex, does subscribe to a certain number of rules and is unlikely to surprise or betray you. The work also provides money, money that can provide comfort and security and can also buy sex. The sex it can buy is, according to Stuart, good sex. And, above all, it is reliable. Stuart produces his own aphorism about love, which he describes as being 'just a system for getting people to call you Darling after sex' (TIO 225). He goes on that, since his promotion to America, he has had sex with a number of prostitutes and has had some girlfriends too: 'I've been to bed with some of them, and some of them have called me Darling, before, afterwards, during. I like that, of course, but I don't trust it. The only Darling I can trust is a Darling I've paid for' (*TIO* 233). Love is unreliable, untrustworthy. It is also a system that works along the same principles as economics, having a value that is 'notional', that is presently 'trading artificially high', and out of which the bottom is about to drop (*TIO* 231). It is important to notice here that what Stuart is describing is not the ways in which love might be subject to the material contingencies that money might produce (when poverty flies in the window, love strides out the door), but the complete immersal of the discourse of love into the discourse of commerce. The effect of this is to alter the nature of love. If discourse is constitutive of the object about which it is apparently talking, then that object will be constituted according to the rules, syntax, and lexicon of that discourse. The 'it' that is being talked over (taken mundanely to mean simply being discussed) is transformed according to how it is being talked about; it is talked over from one realm of discourse into another. This very transformation is itself implicated in the dominant discourse of the market as Oliver demonstrates: '*Make over*. To refashion. But also, in Stuart's mind, a term from the termitic world of business and finance. To make over: to transfer possession (of an object, a title) to someone else. Verb transitive' (*TIO* 104). Love is impossible if the discourse expunges the idiom. The possibility of love that *Talking It Over* seems to be interrogating would appear at this point to be submerged beneath the hegemony of the market.

If the notion of love is constructed from the discourses that seemingly describe it, then so too are individual identities. Identity in the novel is seen as being constructed in two ways. This is either a case of self-representation (that is, talking about oneself *to* an other), or a case of other-presentation (that is, being talked about or to *by* an other). Much of *Talking It Over* plays with the disparity between these two methods of understanding, of knowing, oneself: 'That's the trouble with talking it over like this. It never seems quite right to the person being talked about' (*TIO* 39).

The instability of identity is not only presented structurally (who is the person to whom the characters are talking? How does he or she know so much about them? How is the information transmitted?), but also through the characters' own ruminations on the importance of context in the determining of an identity. Stuart has already demonstrated one aspect of this when he claimed that being in love alters the context of perception. He has remained a frog but that is fine because it is all right to be a frog: love has provided a different and positive context for evaluation. Oliver too has mentioned the transformative power of love, the capacity of love to alter context, when describing Gill's and Stuart's attempts to cheer him up on Frinton beach: 'When people fall in love they develop this sudden resilience, have you noticed? It's not just that nothing can harm them (that old suave illusion), but that nothing can harm anyone they care about either' (*TIO* 46).

Gillian's approach to love is pragmatic. She dismisses the 'old suave illusions' in favour of a practically minded consideration of what love is, what it is capable of doing, and how it needs to be worked at and prepared for. She rejects the grand gesture, preferring instead the mundane and workaday. It is the little gesture that marks out love for Gill, the plausible, the unspectacular.

Gill's pragmatism also requires that she pay attention to context and the ways in which she is defined by context. Unlike Stuart's initial optimism concerning the stability of identity through love (you stay the same, others see you differently), Gill's perception is that identity is created through the discourses that are chosen at any one time. Her identity is seen as one that is structured through its relations with other people and that an alteration in either the structure or the relation will have an impact on the possibilities that ground identity. She recounts a comment by Oliver that seems to encapsulate the different ways in which he and Stuart perceive or interpret her: 'What I meant is merely that for me you are someone of well, endless possibility. I do not stake out and fence in what is taken to be your approved and registered nature' (*TIO* 174). For Gill the question is not which of the two versions of her is most accurate or flattering (determined or endless), but that she is the object of both versions (*TIO* 174).

The attention to context in the recognition of character is also extended to her analyses of others, particularly Oliver, when they have moved to France. Here, again, the capacity of love to evade the contingent, to act as resistance to a specific context, is questioned. The context as a determining factor in the construction or recognition of identity has a necessary effect on the ability to love. It causes the two questions of who am I who is loving, and whom is the person being loved? The context of France makes Gill ask the second of these questions. It is not that she believes Oliver to have changed at all, quite the contrary in fact, but that her perception of this same person has altered. This is different from Stuart's notion of the frog, because in that instance it was love that altered the context of perception. Here it is the context of perception that alters the interpretation of the loved object:

> Oliver's different out here. Actually, I mean the opposite of that. Oliver's exactly the same as he's always been and always will be, it's just that he comes across differently. . . . He needed someone like Stuart around. It's the same as colour theory. When you put two colours side by side, that affects the way you see each of them. It's exactly the same principle. (*TIO* 256)

The context in this case reduces the effect of the person, and he or she seems less impressive than they did before. And, if the loved object is interpreted differently, can the love be the same, can it survive?

The question of the survival of the love between Gill and Oliver is threatened not only by the alteration in context, but, more directly and challengingly by the arrival of Stuart into the village. This, obviously, affects the context primarily by reintroducing a narrative that Gill and Oliver had been trying to suppress – that of the first fifteen chapters. Curiously, it is at this point in the novel, where one loving relationship has already led to the death of love in one of the protagonists, and the other relationship is seen to be in a very fragile state, that love, I will argue, is most powerfully asserted.

Stuart has come to France to seek some sort of revenge, although he is not entirely sure what revenge yet. In a faintly comic attempt at menace, Stuart books into a hotel under a false name: 'I asked for a room at the front. I stand at the window. I watch' (*TIO* 258). What he discovers in his watching is that Oliver and Gill have a baby. In all his correspondence with Gill's mother, Mme Wyatt, she has not told him of this and it comes as a shock almost as great as the initial affair: 'It's reminded me of the future I never got to have. Of everything that was stolen. I'm not sure I can handle this' (*TIO* 261).

Stuart's hoped-for confrontation is stymied by his discovery; he is incapable of making a decision. Gill finds out about the presence of an Englishman in the hotel and just knows that it is Stuart. She immediately recognizes a need for reparation, some sense of obligation for what she has done: 'If he doesn't know [what he wants to do], then I have to give him something, show him something. What? What can I give him?' (*TIO* 264–5).

What she decides upon is the failure of her marriage to Oliver, or rather she decides to stage the failure of her marriage. She already knows that Oliver could be capable of violence towards her, and she knows also that the only thing that is likely to satisfy Stuart's anger is the same thing happening to Oliver and Gill as happened to him. She begins to provoke Oliver with claims that he is having an affair with one of his students, a purposefully improbable choice. This baiting continues all the way through one extremely long night and into the next morning. She carries the baby to the car and continues to shout at Oliver as he is preparing to go to school. Eventually he hits her twice across the face, in full view of Stuart at his window.

What Gill has had to do is to find a way of saying something to Stuart that she does not know how to say. And she has had to say it in an idiom that is heterogeneous to the dominant discourse. She can never tell Oliver of the true cause of her attacks on him, in case he never trusted her again. Because of this, she cannot be certain that what she is staging for Stuart might not turn out to be the truth, that her marriage will fail. What Gill's actions attest to is the obligation to the other – an obligation that can never be recognized as such by the other. And it is that attempt at reparation, that attempt to find an idiom that withstands and flaunts contingency and terror, that is the sign of love.

As in the 'Parenthesis' chapter in *A History of the World in 10½ Chapters*, this love cannot guarantee security, safety, or happiness for any of the people concerned. Stuart, perhaps, is the happiest of the three by the end of the novel, but there is no security in that. Rather, what this love figures is nothing more than its own possibility, a possibility that is capable of resisting the contingent; the banalizing effects of the contemporary. Love as discourse, if it is possible, is always determined by various contextual boundaries that also tend to the suffocation of the idiom of the event. The attempt to breathe the new idiom, as Gill does, is the possibility of love. The possibility of resistance.

8

After the Fall: *The Porcupine*

Published first in Bulgaria as *Bodlivo Svinche* and loosely based on the trial of Bulgarian leader Todor Zhivkov, *The Porcupine* marked a significant departure for Barnes. In many ways this is his most surprising book precisely because in many ways it is not surprising, at least as far as form and structure go. For some critics, Barnes was simply returning to a 'committed' writing that had seen its day and had been done more convincingly by the likes of Orwell, Malraux, and Koestler, with whose *Darkness at Noon* Barnes's novel was unfavourably compared. The novel, however, has far more to offer than these readings would suggest.

Set in a 'sort of Bulgaria',[1] the story told within the novel concerns the trial of Stoyo Petkanov. Petkanov has been 'helmsman of the (un-named) nation for thirty-three years' (*P.* 121). He has been arrested 'quite illegally, without mentioning any charges' (*P.* 9) and is conducting his own defence. His prosecutor is Peter Solinsky. Previously Solinsky had been a member of the Communist Party (which has changed its name to Socialist Party), but is now an official of the new government and member of the Green Party. Solinsky is a proponent of the free market, capitalism, and democracy. Petkanov is an intractable Communist. The trial is therefore both a legal judgement in that an individual is being charged with the violation of specific laws, and a historical judgement in that the individuals are representative of competing modes of political and economic organization and control.

As I have been trying to suggest elsewhere, the narratives that are presented in the works of Barnes are consistently implicated in the manner of their presentation. The primary narrative battle in *The Porcupine* is between Communism and capitalism through the characters of Petkanov and Solinsky. This seemingly crude oppositional framework is subtly employed as an organizing principle in the structure of the novel, but in such a way that an either/or response at the level of structure and thematic is severely problematized, not least by the fact that the initials of the two main characters are the same but in reverse – they are each other's alter ego and as such contain one another.

The narrative of the novel opens with a fable-like quality: 'The old man stood as close to the sixth-floor window as the soldier would allow' (*P.* 1). The character of the old man is introduced as a type. What he is a type of is not entirely obvious: peasant, patriarch, prisoner? It becomes apparent that he is all three of these (and more), but initially Petkanov is an anonymous figure. Despite his generic attribute, the old man is still singularly himself, specifically located inside a multi-storeyed building. This is immediately contrasted with 'Outside', where 'the city was abnormally dark', which itself is contrasted by 'inside, the low wattage of the desk lamp slid thinly from the metal rim of his heavy spectacles' (*P.* 1). Through the window of the room in which he is being held, the old man looks down on the city, the capital city, of the country he had once 'bossed' (*P.* 1) and sees a demonstration being held by the women of the city who are complaining about the food shortages. This demonstration is held wordlessly. The huge noise that accompanies them is the sound of their domestic appliances being banged and clattered; there are no slogans, no chanting, no words at all: 'There was no decline into words, for they had heard nothing but words and words and words – inedible, indigestible words – for months and months and months.' (*P.* 6). It is around the different forms of groups and individuals, insides and outsides, words and wordlessness, public and private, civic and domestic, that the narrative will revolve. These oppositions are themselves organized around the central narrative feature that is the trial of Petkanov, and create a further structural narrative tension between the homogeneous linear narrative of this, and the heterogeneous dispersed events that surround it.

At all levels of the novel there is a refusal to impose one dominating system. Judgement is set up and presented but never practised. The most obvious place where this occurs is in the trial of Petkanov. The fictional account of the trial of Petkanov in the novel addresses the problematic of the form of justice that can be invoked against a person who, from his position of power in a supposedly democratic republican system, has sanctioned the killing of large numbers of other members of that republic. For Prosecutor General Solinsky the task is to provide a justice from within the legal framework that was instituted by Petkanov at the same time as recognizing that, for many of the people watching the trial on the television, the justice that is required is further reaching and extends to the entire communist project. Indeed, one of the possibilities for what form the trial should take is that it be a 'moral trial' (P. 37). There are difficulties with the concept of a moral trial, though. First there is no precedent anywhere in the world for the trial of a whole regime in a criminal court. Related to this point, but exceeding it, is the implied notion of a universal justice – a standard against which all other actions can be measured. It is to this notion that one of the students who is watching the televised trial seems to appeal. Dimiter, the student, complains about the treatment of Petkanov, protesting not only that the charges are trivial, but that the trial is being too nice to him. For the students, and particularly for Dimiter, Petkanov is guilty of 'mass murder', 'genocide', 'ruining the country' (P. 32). This is self-evident and allows for no ambivalence – he has committed crimes against humanity.

For Solinsky, the problem is that, even if Petkanov is guilty of a broad conception of criminality that can be defined as morally unjust, without firm evidence it is impossible justly to convict him – and firm evidence is very difficult for Solinsky to come by.

Solinsky's opportunity to prove Petkanov guilty comes, at last, when a memorandum is presented to him by his adviser. It has apparently been initialled by, authorized by, Petkanov and states that saboteurs should be 'discouraged by all necessary means' (P. 91). This would suggest that Petkanov sanctioned, or at least knew about, the murder of dissidents. Along with this discovery is the proof that a substance had been developed, again it would seem with Petkanov's full knowledge and support, that could be used to kill political opponents by simulating the effects of a cardiac arrest. Added to this is the documentation relating to the Minister of Culture, Anna Petkanova – Petkanov's own daughter – who was deemed to be damaging the Communist cause by her extravagance, and who died mysteriously of a heart attack. With these three strands of evidence, Solinsky begins to think he has an irrefutable case. He enters the courtroom with confidence, delivers his evidence and sums up in exuberant style (P. 110–11).

Solinsky's exuberance is marred by his brutal pragmatism:

> If Petkanov hadn't signed that memorandum, he must have signed something like it. We are only putting into concrete form an order he must have given over the telephone. Or with a handshake, a nod, a pertinent failure to disapprove. The document is true, even if it is a forgery. Even if it isn't true, it is necessary. Each excuse was weaker, yet also more brutal. (P. 113)

In *The Porcupine* everybody knows that Petkanov's regime committed acts of embezzlement, murder, torture, and more. This is common knowledge, but there is no documentary proof, no eye-witness accounts, no orders, no photographs, no receipts, no taped telephone calls. There is nothing until the discovery of the memorandum that is supposed to have been signed by Petkanov. In order for justice to be done, documents are forged and are given the status of truths: fakes, forgeries, and lies are the platforms for a justice that is supposed to be condemning fakes, forgeries, and lies. This, however, is to overdetermine the reading, for it is by no means obvious that the documents are forged; it certainly seems probable that they are, but this simply leaves, again, one probabilistic discourse battling against another probabilistic discourse.

This is the same with the trial itself, and the seeming triumph of capitalism. This triumph is not universally welcomed. The old grandmother of one of the group of students watching the trial is a solitary figure at the end of the novel, silently clinging to her beliefs and holding a small framed portrait of Lenin in her hand. This is where the novel ends and it is structurally a very important section. A comparison of the final paragraph with the first paragraph demonstrates how carefully the resonances and almost-oppositions in the novel have been set up. As with Petkanov in the first paragraph, the grandmother is presented generically: 'In front of the vacant Mausoleum of the First Leader an old woman stood alone' (*P.* 138). The old woman is, like Petkanov, a Communist. She is also old. Unlike Petkanov, she is silent when abused. To some extent, then, there is a pleasing circularity to the narrative, with the story being bracketed by two old Communists illumined by thin light. The resonances that are thrown up, however, subtly disrupt this easy symmetry. The old woman, in her silence and pride, is as much related to the huge demonstration of women at the beginning of the novel as she is to Petkanov, and they in turn have an affinity with the Devinsky Commandos. The Devinsky Commandos are a small group of demonstrators whose political strategy is cynical ironic disruption. In the months leading up to the overthrow of Petkanov, wearing the too-small headgear of the Communist youth, the Devinskys would chant a variety of witheringly caustic phrases at the offices of certain administrative centres. Among their repertoire is the pleasing little triplet:

'THANK YOU FOR THE PRICE RISES.'
'THANK YOU FOR THE FOOD SHORTAGES.'
'GIVE US IDEOLOGY NOT BREAD.' (*P.* 46)

After the fall of the Communists they continue their disruption with a mock auction of Petkanov's goods and shackles, and a postcard sent to Solinsky after the prosecution that states 'Give us convictions not justice' (*P.* 127). In their detachment, refusal to adopt a serious political orthodoxy, and determined irony, the Devinsky Commandos are perhaps the only political and moral alternative to those offered elsewhere in the novel.

The activities of the Devinsky Commandos are different from those of the group of students who are returned to throughout the novel, and of one of whom the old woman is grandmother. The students act almost like a chorus, commenting on the main action of the trial and adding their own opinions and ideas. For Vera, one of the students, there is a responsibility on them 'to be witnesses' (*P.* 19), and their witnessing occurs via the television.

The trial scenes are written as if the narrator is in the courtroom, with detailed third-person descriptions of the surroundings and proceedings. An apposite example of this is the description of the courtroom:

> The courtroom had been built in an early-Seventies mode of softened brutalism: pale wood, flattened angles, chairs that approached comfort. It could have been a rehearsal theatre, or a small concert hall in which spiky wind quintets were played, except for the lighting, a drab collaboration of strip neon and cowled down-lamps. It gave no favouritism or focus; the effect was flat, democratic, unjudging. (*P.* 30)

Apart from the way in which the description of the room stands to some extent for an account of the novel in its emphasis on the lack of favouritism or judgement (an analogy that should not be extended too far), and also the way that this linkage is playfully executed with the trading-off of images (a 'spiky' wind quartet in a book called *The Porcupine* is an act worthy of minor celebration), this passage also illustrates the knowingness of the narrator. God-eyed and knowledgeable, the narrative voice appears to provide an absolute and authoritative account of the narrative.

The narratorial stability that this might be thought to provide is, however, disrupted by the bracketed, italicized comments of the students. While we are *told of* the disruptive, cynical activities of the Devinsky Commandos, we are literally presented with the disruptive potential of the students. Their comments act both as stringent attacks on the old regime and as caustic rejoinders to the supposed benefits of the new system. When Solinsky reads out the list of charges, the students' own list stands in terrible juxtaposition:

> 'mismanagement under Article 332 (8) of the Penal Code.'
> (*'Mismanagement!'*
> *'Mismanagement of the prison camps.'*
> *'He didn't torture people properly enough.'*
> *'Shit. Shit.'*)
> 'How do you plead?' (*P.* 32)

Simply at the level of typography, the novel demonstrates the ways in which the boundaries of communication are being dissolved by new technologies. Two discrete events – the legal trial of the former leader of a country and the gathering together of a group of students in a flat – can be linked in ways that refuse the monolithic discourses of homogenization. Groups of phrases, chains of events that are foreign to each other, are open to the free circulation of accidental linkage. This, however, is not to suppose that the free circulation of discourses is in any way identical with free-market capitalism. Access to the multiplicity of language games that comes with the defeat of Communism is not a guarantee of any greater justice. Petkanov had made a similar point earlier, drawing on the symbolic economy of postmodernity:

> It all started with Frank Sinatra, the whole fucking thing. Sinatra fucked Nancy Reagan in the White House, that's what they said, didn't they? Reagan couldn't control his wife. Nancy had a dressing-up competition with Raisa. Gorbachev couldn't control *his* wife. And Gorbachev's spokesman says we're all going to follow the Sinatra Doctrine. The Elvis Presley Doctrine. The McDonald's Hamburger Doctrine. The Doctrine of Mickey Mouse and Donald Duck. (P. 19)

The imperative of the symbolic to the Communist regime, and the imperative of the appropriation or denial of the symbol by its opponents, is matched by the desire to literalize metaphors, to actualize symbolic speech, as seen in many exchanges between Petkanov and Solinsky.

The battle over symbols, institutional or anecdotal, is recognized by Bulgarian writer Ivailo Dichev in his story 'Desires: The Erotica of Communism'. Towards the end of this short story there is a small section called 'Literalisms' that concludes with the following paragraph:

> If Communism was a literalization of metaphors (that the cook must lead the country, that the people will be brothers when everything is taken from them . . .), its fall was no less literal. The Berlin Wall fell. Anyone can buy a piece as a souvenir. The masses invaded Romanian television. We saw them cluster there needlessly before the screen, as if they wanted to participate directly, physically in history. Words were assaulted, articles of the constitution were besieged. The five-pointed star, mummies and statues were attacked. Literalism has been defeated. Literally.[2]

Peter Solinsky is engaged in the attempt to refuse the literalization of symbol and story by recasting these efforts as cheap analogy. The text refuses either position superiority, inscribing the battle instead as an open-ended interpretative play where the monolithic discourses of Communism are fragmented, dispersed.

As was mentioned earlier, this is also Barnes's textual strategy. Despite the knowingness of the narratorial voice, the narrative itself is undecidable. The juxtapositions are weighted in such a way that it is not possible to judge which, if any, of the characters, narratives, or symbols is pre-eminent. What we are presented with is the balancing of differences that are irreducible to each other and also irresolvable in respect of truth.

Between Petkanov and Solinsky, between Communism and capitalism, there is a huge gulf. There does, however, exist a space for a tribunal; neither ideology seeks as a point of principle the exclusion of communication with those it considers its enemies. Yet where this tribunal can be found is a different problem. The symbolic trial of a leader of a Communist country, under the rules of the old regime but with an explicitly opposed ideological agenda, and with the use of forged evidence, does not seem even to come close. One place where the tribunal has occurred, of course, is in the pages of the novel. This novelistic tribunal has not been an arena where truth and falsehood have been defined nor has it been one where one could draw a verdict in favour of either of the competing individuals, political systems, discursive genres, narratives of emancipation, nationhood, or individuality. What it has been an arena of is justice.

Any verdict has to be a judgement by the reader, a judgement that, moreover, is sensitive to the demands and dangers of such a judgement. Without any final verdict to be given, the novel has engaged in a dialogue, a conversation, with the competing systems, but a dialogue that has not attempted to provide a consensus.

The silence of the grandmother at the end of the novel demonstrates this impossible judgement. It is said of her that, 'whatever the words, she stood her ground, and she remained silent' (*P.* 138). Unlike the ironic gestures of the Devinsky Commandos, the grandmother's silence is a complete detachment from the processes of political democracy and its language of rights. Her detached silence is both demanded *and* abhorred by democracy. It is demanded to the extent that she represents that which must be defeated and silenced in order for capital democracy to succeed (Communism). But it is abhorred because democratic capitalism demands, precisely, the *voicing* of differences. This freedom of speech that denotes democracy is seen, though, not just as a right but as an obligation. One is obliged to speak freely – failure to do so is to deny oneself rights.

The grandmother, in refusing to speak, is both absenting herself from democratic justice and critiquing it, at the same time as being denied access to its procedures and benefits.

In *The Porcupine* Barnes has written a novel that demands of its readers that they examine the limits of their own notions of justice in a context that is determined by, and that bears directly on, all of our lives – the political history of the contemporary.

9

An Island of the Time Before: *England, England*

Between the publication of *The Porcupine* in 1991 and *England, England* in 1998 there had been no other Barnes novels. The intervening period had seen a selection of journalistic articles drawn from Barnes's writing for the *New Yorker* called *Letters from London* (1995) and a collection of short stories, *Cross Channel* (1996). Both of these, in different ways, had addressed the notion of Englishness, and so it was not, perhaps, surprising that the new novel should also be an attempt to engage with questions of English identity and history. What was perhaps more surprising, from an author whose works had previously seemed so fresh and new, was the extent to which the novel also seemed to rehearse ideas and themes already encountered in previous of his novels in a fashion that was also very similar to earlier treatments.

The novel is written in three sections. The first and third sections are comparatively short and recount the life of Martha Cochrane. In section one, 'England', we see a recollection of her life as a child in the England of the late twentieth century and in section three, 'Anglia', we see her living the life of an 'old maid' in the England (or Anglia as it is now called) of the mid-twenty-first century. The middle and longer section, 'England, England', tells the tale of Sir Jack Lupton's invention of a tourist England relocated to the Isle of White (now called England, England). Martha, in this section, is part of the team that helps to instigate and finally implement the audacious scheme.

A problem with the novel, even from this very bald account, is that the three sections do not really cohere. It is as if there is one story about the growth of a young woman into adulthood and then old age, and another story about the invention of a tourist England that allows for a number of themes pertinent to contemporary debates about authenticity and history. In itself this might not be a major criticism: after all, Barnes's work has always pushed the possibilities of narrative and structure, but, in this case, the pushing seems to have torn the fabric. In the discussion of *A History of the World in 10½ Chapters*, I suggest that the novel enacts its own critique at the level of the failure of art, and that this is a triumph of the novelist. Here, however, there is the suspicion that, in trying to make the novel enact the themes of which it is talking, what one ends up with is a rather predictable, and even tired, piece of work.

The 'England, England' section, which I shall come to in more detail shortly, concerns itself with Sir Jack's idea of recreating on the Isle of White all of those aspects of England that seek to encapsulate its history and identity. Included within this are the Royal Family, Robin Hood, Manchester United Football Club, historic buildings, natural features, and so on. Each of these will be remade in an environment that allows for easy access, comfort, hospitality, and ease. One of the dominant themes, then, that arises from this is the extent to which the original has any more or less value than the remade version: authenticity versus simulacra. In an interview with Penelope Dening, Barnes was eager to insist that, despite the fact that the idea for *England, England* sounds implausible, it does have genuine, real-world, analogues: 'I've taken some liberties, but if you think that there is a Las Vegas hotel chain planning to recreate the centre of Venice, the Doge's Palace, the Campanile, it's completely logical'.[1]

With so much discussion about borrowing, quotation, pastiche, fraud, originality, and so on, it is almost inevitable that a reader will, however unwillingly, begin to make connections or ask questions about the novel's own relationship to each of these ideas. And, in the opinion of this writer, the conclusions are not good. *England, England*, in many respects, reads like the miniaturized, condensed, safe, easily accessible island world of Barnes's other books. Andrew Marr, in contrast to this position, claims that the book 'is both ambitious and serious – real, if you like'.[2] However, even in interview it sounded as though

73

Barnes was culling his earlier works. Again with Penelope Dening, Barnes explains what it is that spurs him to write. He suggests that he has itches and that these need scratching. The 'itches' for this novel were 'love, truth, integrity, stuff like that'.[3] Step back twenty years and you hear Chris from *Metroland* claiming to find in art 'a clutch of capitalised intangibles like Love, Truth, Authenticity' (*M.* 15). Life imitating art imitating life . . .

Structurally the novel returns to the triptych organization of *Metroland* and, more pertinently, *Staring at the Sun*. As with *Staring at the Sun*, the main character is a woman looking back on her life. Not only that, Martha looks back and asks pretty much the same questions as Jean and arrives at pretty much the same sorts of answers. Martha ponders memory and, in contradistinction to her questioners, answers 'it wasn't like any of that' (*EE* 3 (the first page of the novel)). Jean ponders memory and in contradistinction to her questioners replies 'It wasn't like that' (*SS* 5 (the first page of the novel)). Martha is very clever but regarded with suspicion and hostility by some; Jean is dull and plodding and regarded with condescension. Both approach old age with a certain stoic disappointment, both have nearly had lesbian affairs, both have been bruised by love, and both have a childhood memory that motivates later narrative moments – the jigsaw of the counties of England and a book from a childhood fête in Martha's case.

The deftly crafted discussion of jazz in *Staring at the Sun*, with its light self-reflexive overtones, becomes a heavy-handed knowingness in *England, England* with discussion of 'ironic post-post-modernism' (*EE* 29), which comes at the end of a discussion of architecture that is also conspicuously overstated, unlike the marvellous modulations found, for example, in *The Porcupine*. Martha's 'Brief History of Sexuality' is an obvious reflection back on *A History of the World in 10½ Chapters* (replete with parenthesis), and bears no little resemblance to the list Gregory makes regarding the possible existence of God in *Staring at the Sun*. Gregory's model aeroplane from *Staring at the Sun* finds a curious metaphorical reprise on p. 43. Martha's father left her mother when Martha was young, as Gill's father, in *Talking It Over*, left her mother when Gill was young, an event that subsequent people want to foist significance onto. Like all of Barnes's women, Martha either wants or is supposed to represent simplicity, honesty, and truth, and then becomes the object of complaint, or complains herself, if this is not the case. When talking to herself about her relationship with Paul, she concludes, 'No, it feels like this: no games, no deceptions, no pretence, no betrayal' (*EE* 97), which could have been spoken by Gill or Jean or been attributed to Marion in *Metroland*. Despite her resemblance to many other characters, Martha 'is one of (Barnes') best achievements', according to Maggie Gee.[4] Apart from Martha, there are also other strong resonances (before we even approach the thematic level), not least between the historian Dr Max and Oliver from *Talking It Over*. The clever, witty, learned self-absorbed vignettes and *bon mots* seem laboured by comparison with the more flamboyant predecessor.

These comparisons are not here simply to chastise this novel, but to suggest that it might be possible to claim that Barnes, in *England, England*, is himself deploying the strategies of simulacra, inauthenticity, and fake in order to tell a story of simulacra, inauthenticity, and fake. However, if this is so, then the experiment does not work. Independently of the worries concerning the mining of one's own previous works for current ideas in such a blatant form (postmodern self-referential pastiche might be one way of describing it), there is the more particular factor that the two stories do not meld together. Barnes himself is aware of the difficulty in making the sections cohere: 'The technical difficulty of the book is actually marrying those extremes of tonality and trying to get them to work together'.[5]

It seems clear that the long middle section requires a 'before' and 'after' to contextualize the debates and impact of 'England, England'. It also seems to make sense to locate these around a character who straddles all three sections and who has some genuine investment in the project of England, England itself. Martha's childhood in Old England and old age in Anglia appear, then, to provide a neat structuring principle. However, the shift in focus between the two sections is such that the hoped-for comparison seems forced.

Section one is very localized. Martha's childhood is remembered around three prominent areas. These are: the jigsaw of the counties of England that her father helps her with; the fête that she attends; and her father's leaving her and her mother. The jigsaw is a handy metaphor for the idea of a country being constructed, arbitrarily divided into administrative centres, historically open to change, and so on. Also, the fact that her father also keeps one piece hidden from her so that she can never finish the puzzle operates as a beautifully crafted emotional metaphor that is used to full effect when she meets him after a number of years and he cannot remember the jigsaw, let alone the particular piece that he left with. Martha's upset and anger are deftly and touchingly shown. The memory of the fête, her desire to grow beans, the list of the categories of entries for the agricultural show all have a thematic and emotional vitality that set Martha up as a character with particular strengths and weaknesses, specific predilections and occupations of mind. More generally, the ways in which the memories are recounted or even remembered (however in-debted to Jean Serjeant they may be) serve as interesting precursors to what the reader may hope is to come. The aching uncertainty and desire for truth are subtly handled here, and perhaps nowhere more pithily than in the short aside when she remembers sitting at a table watching her mother cry – 'and this was a true, single, unprocessed memory, she was sure of that, she was almost sure of that' (*EE* 14).

The Martha of the final section also goes to a fête, grows beans, lives in a rural environment, and so on, but the closely observed details of section one have given way to a vast, broad canvas on which a whole history of a country after a certain point is presented. This is, of course, a necessary attempt: what happens to England after England, England? But the novel has spent so long positing different notions of history, and chal-lenging many assumptions about history, that this brief chron-icle is pretty much self-defeating. Despite the claim that 'this marked the start of the second period, over which future historians would long disagree' (*EE* 252), there is a brazen lack of complexity or doubt about the history supposedly being represented. And much of the 'first period', even in a satirical novel, stretches credulity to the point where even the satire struggles to impress. This point is made most forcibly by Andrew Marr, who claims that, by the final section, 'Barnes's satire had curdled into self pity'.[6] This, though, is thematically interesting only if the linking point has maintained interest, and Martha has dwindled by now. She has noticed that 'the operation of memory was becoming more random' (*EE* 242), and a little later we hear: 'old England had lost its history, and therefore – since memory is identity – had lost all sense of self' (*EE* 251). Martha's random memory and Anglia's lost identity become one and the same symptom of a book that seems to have lost its way. Even Barnes's usual verbal flair appears to have been somewhat blunted by the ever-increasing self-referentiality of the novel. Referring back to the list from section one, Martha tries to provide some sense of what a village fête might include in terms of competition entries for an agricultural fair. In a pleasing moment the list is rejected because it seems to indicate a civilization that was complicated and 'decadent' (*EE* 247). The delightfully askance idea of the decadence of carrots is bewilderingly muddled only seven pages later when, in a list of the wonders of a replenished nature excused the punishment of industrialization, the newly thriving quince and mulberry are also described as 'decadent' (*EE* 255). Whether this is intended to show an aesthetic and moral permeability, a shift in narrative voice, the variable nature of the sign or whatever, it remains the fact the word interrupts the reading in a fashion that does not seem to advance the novel.

It is in the long central section that the main aspects of the novel occur. This is the effort by Sir Jack Pitman, self-styled 'entrepeneur, innovator, ideas man, arts patron, inner-city revitaliser' (*EE* 29), to provide for his monumental career one last, huge achievement: his version of Beethoven's Ninth. Pitman is clearly a cartoon-figure representation of the likes of Maxwell and Murdoch, a cartoon that Lucy Kellaway, a writer with the *Financial Times*, feels to be unfair. While, in an article for the Internet magazine *Prospect*, she chastises Barnes for the easy slip into stereotype and cliché with regard to big business, she nevertheless points out that, with the possible exception of David Lodge, almost no English novelist in the last half of the twentieth century even attempted to write a business novel.[7]

Pitman's idea is the development of 'England, England', the newly created theme park on the Isle of White that houses all of the tourist attractions associated with what we come to recognize as old England. Sir Jack has a body of people who work for him, of whom one is Martha Cochrane. Her job is to voice opposition and contrast to the assembly of yes-men who otherwise make up his staff. Martha proves her worth during interview by being witty, obstinate, and above all cynical: 'It's as true as you want it to be. If it suits, it's true. If not, I'll change it' is her response to a question concerning the accuracy of her application (*EE* 45).

In many respects, cynicism is the abiding motif of this section of the novel. From Sir Jack's justifications for his drive for power, to Dr Max's fey irritation at the ignorance of the populace, to Paul's collaboration in the blackmail of Sir Jack and subsequent repudiation of Martha, all of the major characters display a moral life predicated on the cynical manipulation of circumstance. Also, they make use of the fact that the circumstances themselves appear to be so malleable and unstable. When there is nothing real, there is no need to apologize for manipulation.

While the novel in some respects is a corrosive critique of what may be thought to be England, it is as much a consideration of the 'what may be thought to be'. Indeed, the very phrasing of that last sentence, with its almost obligatory quotation marks, is itself interrogated in the novel. When one of the actors on England, England becomes too involved in his character, this is partly described as being the responsibility of the island for having peeled off 'the protective quotation marks and leaving him vulnerable' (*EE* 217). The quotation of history, of people, of places, of things, this is what England, England is all about. It celebrates the duplicate, the model, the inauthentic. Sir Jack's bold move was to believe the claims of post-modern theory, or of contemporary sociological analysis, and to create a venue where history is represented as a series of cosy simulacra, even down to having a meal with Dr Johnson, or 'Dr Johnson', of an evening.

The question of simulacra, of the relative merit of the real versus the copy, the very possibility of there being a real in the first place, have been the mainstay of much contemporary theory and philosophizing. Translating some of these often obscure and difficult arguments into novelistic form here has the effect of sometimes banalizing the arguments, and sometimes obscuring the novel. The most sustained account of theoretical arguments is presented by, appropriately enough, a French intellectual bought in by Sir Jack to join his team at the beginning of the project. While the exposition is certainly a reasonable pastiche of a sort of postmodern theory, it sits uneasily here. Partly, it is difficult to see Sir Jack bothering to find academic justification in the first place (an idea borne out by his dropping of the fee later), but mainly because it reads like a lesson that Barnes himself is proud to have learned so well, but rather embarrassed to have included, which might account for the barbed introduction it receives from the narrator:

> But with a few suave gestures he drew doves from his sleeve and a line of flags from his mouth. Pascal led to Saussure via Laurence Sterne: Rousseau to Baudrillard via Edgar Allen Poe, the Marquis de Sade, Jerry Lewis, Dexter Gordon, Bernard Hinault and the early work of Anne Sylvestre; Levi-Strauss led to Levi-Strauss. (*EE* 53)

The mad mix of seemingly disparate characters drawn together in a vaguely specious line of argument is not new to postmodern theory and it is wittily debunked here. However, the novel's own use of the theory it debunks fares no better. Sir Jack is doubtless being parodied when he asks and proceeds to answer the question 'What is real?' (*EE* 31), but the parody itself runs the risk of being as dull and irritating as the poor fifth-form philosophy it intends to criticize. This becomes more evident as the novel constantly draws attention to questions of a similar ilk, posing problems about the true and the false, appearance versus reality, the status of art in a consumerist society, nature versus culture in a number of increasingly obtrusive ways. Paul, trying to read Sir Jack's face, leaves the narrator to comment, 'though whether such complexities of emotion in fact existed was another matter' (*EE* 32). Sir Jack calls all his secretaries Susie, so 'it was not really her name he was unsure of but her identity' (*EE* 34). Pitman's consultant is the Batson in 'Cabot, Albertazzi and Batson', although the other two members do not exist; it is all for presentation, like the snuff that is 'really' darkened cocaine. Sir Jack engages in some cultural theory while walking and discovers that no one just 'walked' any more, if they ever did, for the sheer pleasure. It was and always had been a business venture. By the same token, nature was not 'nature' but man-made (*EE* 40–4).

The preamble to the making of England, England is itself the rehearsal of a number of ideas concerning the propensity of the contemporary to prefer the imitation over the original. In addition, the economic and political arguments that go along with some of these ideas (mass-market reproductions produce a democratization of culture/mass-market reproductions produce a paucity of knowledge) are also rehearsed. They are presented, mostly, as set-piece vignettes that stand alone.

The England that will be most successful as a tourist operation is based on a wide-scale market research survey that itself masquerades as something to do, obscurely, with a soft drinks company. The example we are presented with is easily enough compartmentalized into specific categories by the researcher (age, sex, nationality, and so on), and his lack of knowledge with regard to the details of the Battle of Hastings is amusing enough and will doubtless chasten one or two readers of the novel. From such surveys Dr Max, the team's official historian, learns a number of things. One of these is that 'patriotism's most eager bedfellow was ignorance, not knowledge' (*EE* 82), and the other is the fifty quintessences of Englishness.

The difficulty the novel seems to have here is that there is not much in the way of story in which to fit these ruminations and speculations. The novel provides a range of characters who may just about plausibly contemplate these ideas, but there is not really the venue for them to be aired in, apart from board meetings.

Perhaps as a consequence of this, perhaps for other reasons, the narrative becomes blend of failed love story, company coup, test of loyalty, and character revelation. The love story between Martha and Paul, another employee of the Lipton corporation, is pleasant enough, but seems to serve only to elucidate an earlier Barnes notion of love: 'That was the word: falling in love with Martha made things more real' (*EE* 103). The next phase of the love story is the slow realization from both of them that being more real does not mean being happier and the slow decline into distance and suspicion is not long in coming. One of its motors is the event that had seemed to unite them in the first place: the blackmail of Sir Jack after they discover that he has a sexual fetish for dressing as a baby and defecating. The self-proclaimed family man is seen to be not all he may have appeared – not altogether surprising in a book such as this.

Sir Jack's desire to maintain the image of himself that has been created through his achievements and self-publicity means that he relinquishes control of the company to Martha, although she had never seemed to have any desire either for power for its own sake, or for this particular manifestation of it. Paul becomes increasingly distanced from her and retains a respect for Sir Jack that eventually leads him to side with Sir Jack and oust Martha.

This attempt to produce a story around which the other events of *England, England* can unfold is unconvincing. The characters' motivations do not seem to coincide with their actions. Again, this may be an attempt by Barnes to demonstrate how unfixed and surprising people can be, but the execution of this idea, if such it is, does not fulfil its ambition.

The essayist of *Letters from London* could have written convincingly on the themes of simulacra, Englishness, and the contemporary state of theory. The short-story writer of *Cross Channel* could have written a number of tales that included the same characters in more condensed situations. The novelist, in trying to do both things at once, for once failed to produce a novel that moved and provoked. Its inclusion on the Booker Prize shortlist remains, for me, at least, a mystery.

10

Ending up from Paris in
London: *Love, etc. and
Conclusion*

At the publication of *Cross Channel*, Barnes was interviewed by
Salon Internet magazine. According to the interviewer, Carl
Swanson, Barnes professed ignorance as to the World Wide
Web, and, after considering its implications for a royalties-
based publishing system, decided that he was not in favour of
the idea that 'Information wants to be free'.[1] This phrase
becomes one of the figures around which Stuart Hughes
constructs his telling of events in Barnes's last novel to date,
Love, etc. This novel is a return to the characters and form of
Talking It Over and the fact that it includes a reference to an
interview from the mid-1990s suggests, as Barnes makes clear
in a BBC interview, that the earlier novel had continued to
fascinate Barnes: 'form drew me back and the characters were
still alive.'[2]

If, as I suggested earlier, *England, England* is a rerun of earlier
themes and ideas, then *Love, etc*. is an explicit sequel. This is
not a term favoured by Barnes, but it is what the novel is. In
many ways, this is a useful coincidence for the critic, as it
allows me the freedom to use that novel as a concluding point
in this study. Any effort to draw a line under Barnes's work
would obviously be fruitless: he continues to write and is likely
to publish either another collection of themed stories or a
selection of essays on French subjects shortly. However, it does
seem reasonable to use *Love. etc*. as a moment of summary and
assessment. This is not, I hasten to add, a claim that there is an

œuvre that can be assessed as this word and its attendant implications have a rather morbid signification for Barnes ('It suggests I'm dead . . .').[3]

This novel is a much darker treatment of similar themes to those found in *Talking It Over*, themes concerned with questions of truth, subjectivity, and love. In one way or another these have dominated Barnes's novels from the outset and it is a testament to his virtuosity that he can not only keep making them seem lively, new, and urgent, but that he can do this while repeating a form already employed by him. However, it is also true to say that *Love. etc.* is more than simply a sequel. It continues the characters' stories from *Talking It Over*, but it also draws clearly and self-consciously from his other novels, too. Unlike *England, England*, though, this novel manages to draw his earlier works into the main concerns of this one without overshadowing or undermining the present story.

The story of *Love. etc.* is that Stuart has returned from the United States, where he has married and divorced, and is in England to set up an organic food company. Gillian and Oliver have moved back to London, after their time in France, and now have another daughter. Gill is still a picture restorer, and Oliver is a would-be screen-writer. Stuart gets back in contact with his ex-best friend and ex-wife, gives Oliver a job, and arranges for the family to move into the house where he and Gill lived when they were first married. The darkness stems from Stuart's continuing obsession with Gill, his sustained resentment and irritation with Oliver; from Oliver's previous and present nervous breakdowns; from Sophie's (the elder daughter) anorexia; from the seduction-cum-rape of Gillian by Stuart; from Terri (Stuart's American ex-wife) describing Stuart in America with his photograph of the bleeding and bruised Gill; and from each of the characters being less happy, more frustrated , less alive than in the first book.

These descriptions all bear on one of the main aspects of the novel, which is betrayal. This is set up early on, where Stuart clearly asserts: 'Trust leads to betrayal' (*LE* 12). Throughout the novel each of the main characters has a betrayal with which to contend: Oliver finds out that Stuart witnessed his hitting of Gill and that, therefore, Gill had orchestrated the event. Stuart then discovers the same thing, that the event was staged for his benefit. Gill's sense of betrayal is after the sex/rape that she endures. Even Mme Wyatt, Gill's mother, expresses her sense of betrayal and the bitterness this develops:

> I desire bitterly and without cease, to be young again . . . I desire not to die. I desire also to die in my sleep . . . I also desire that my husband, who betrayed me, suffer because of it. Sometimes I go to church and pray. I am not a believer, but I pray that there is a God and that in another life my husband be punished as a sinner. I want him to burn in the hell I do not believe in.
>
> So you see, I also have hard feelings. You are very naïve about us, the old people. (*LE* 144)

What this passage helps to demonstrate, apart from the bleakness of much of the novel and the centrality of betrayal and desire, is a novelist at the top of his trade. Amid the bitterness, there is the attenuated humour to be derived from Mme Wyatt's ailing grasp of English (a deterioration spotted by Oliver earlier on), as well as the fusing of themes.

Apart from the domestic concerns of the characters, the novel is also interrogating the loss of faith and the lack of myth in the contemporary world. Mme Wyatt's lament about her husband touches on this loss as part of her diatribe. But it is as an aspect of her character that this is developed. Where, in *England, England*, theme had dominated and obliterated character as anything other than a caricature, here the theme and the characters develop together, with the movement of the one being counterpointed by the movement of the other.

It is with this degeneration of structures of belief that the remainder of this concluding section will deal. As I hope to have demonstrated elsewhere, Barnes's novels are distinct productions linked by certain qualities of narrative invention and thematic concern. One of these concerns, indeed perhaps the major one under which all the others are being scrutinized in story form, is the loss of faith. This phrase is very broad, but includes at a very general level the loss of hope once promised by art (*Metroland, A History of the World in 10½ Chapters*); the failure of religion (*A History of the World in 10½ Chapters, Staring at the Sun*), the possibilities of science and technology (*Before She Met Me, Staring at the Sun, A History of the World in 10½ Chapters*); the claims of politics (*Metroland, A History of the*

World in 10½ Chapters, The Porcupine, England, England); an idea of history (*Metroland, Before She Met Me, Flaubert's Parrot, Staring at the Sun, A History of the World in 10½ Chapters, The Porcupine, England, England*), a commitment to the idea of self (*Before She Met Me, Flaubert's Parrot, Staring at the Sun*); and even the practical effect of love – all of the novels.

The bleakness of *Love. etc.* derives not only from each of the characters' own personal torments, but also because these torments are linked by the characters to broader concerns regarding the loss of faith, the lack of any structures within which to place themselves, the collapse of the sustaining metaphysical categories.

The most persistent pessimist in this sense is Oliver. Professionally unfulfilled, depressive, and believing the last ten years to have been a lived lie, he is perhaps the most likely candidate to seek redemption through other means. Not having a religious faith, Oliver seeks meaning through literary and artistic history, aesthetics, and the speculative paradigms he can talk himself into through these. From these he can build a tentative world view, a morality that provides, however fragile, a position from which he can make sense and make judgements. Discussing the tangle of relationships between the characters, he likens each telling of their stories to a novel (and observes that Stuart's is unpublishable). From this he is able to discern a moral pattern that he claims the reader will say is 'all a matter of degree, and I will reply: no, it is a matter of absolutes' (*LE* 14).

Oliver's absolutist moral order is never more than a rhetorical flourish, however, and his delight in making 'pretty patterns with words' (*LE* 221) leads him into a position of extreme scepticism and doubt that, ultimately, makes his world banal and, because banal, unbearable. This is demonstrated early on when he is thinking about marriage and surmises that men marry for a number of reasons but that lead among these is that 'what they truly seek is their conscience' (*LE* 77). The idea that love's apotheosis, marriage, is simply a convenient tool for soul cleansing might be deemed to be saddening, but Oliver goes a step further in his idea and claims: 'Or might it, alternatively, be that this is not what men truly seek but what marriage, of necessity, turns women into?

85

Now that would be rather more banal. Not to mention more tragic' (*LE* 77). Oliver admits that some of his philosophical conclusions are rather 'DIY' (*LE* 32) and, one would have to add, rather eclectically drawn. He finds his above hypothesis 'tragic', yet it is precisely the lack of tragic figures, of grand themes, of overarching and powerful forces that he bemoans. He recognizes a world without a god or gods, and is unable to locate himself in it, except as a figure of despair.

It is Stuart who provides Oliver with a fragmentary explanatory focus. Stuart, the plodding, mercantile businessman who is also malign benefactor, is not the obvious candidate for a phrase about which Oliver can say, 'What metaphysician, what moralist could put it better?' (*LE* 73). The phrase is 'The law of unintended effect' and is more properly related to questions of ecological accident, yet Oliver translates it into the language of belief, however distressing that belief is:

> I regard it as a true expression of the tragic principle of life. Those old gods are dead, and little Johnny Quark is a grey-suited Stuart of a creation in my book, but the Law of Unintended Effect, now that is grand, that is Greek, that instructs us how mighty is the gap between invention and deed, between purpose and consequence, how vain our striving proves, how precipitate and Luciferian our fall. We are all, are we not, lost? (*LE* 73)

Oliver finds his metaphor for his life, his explanatory principle, but all it does is to confirm his general despair, his loss of faith. Not even his skill at literary introjection provides him with a salve, as he realizes that the stories that might provide comfort or purpose work only in a culture that still maintains its propensity for mythic (even fabled) truth. Myth made being a pawn a mighty role, for Oliver, 'when there were knights and bishops and kings on the board, when a pawn might dream of becoming a queen, when there was black and white, and God above' (*LE* 85). But the certainties of well-drawn adversaries, of good and evil, are gone: 'There is no either/or, there is only both/and' (*LE* 186). Oliver laments the loss of this mythic 'either/or' certainty. This certainty is not the minor truth of realism, which is simply the brute acceptance of mundanity and the failure of change. Hoping to find solace in fable, Oliver is disappointed because he realizes 'the world, being constructed as it is, will not allow it. Realism is our given, our only mode, *triste* truth as it might come to some.' The fable is false because hares are faster than and cleverer than tortoises. Any other mode (and here he borrows from Geoffey Braithwaite in his discussion of literary genres) is a lie (*LE* 156).

Oliver desires truth, a system of belief, a mythic universe in which right and wrong, true and false, can be articulated, where portents signify calamitous events rather than 'becoming more local [with] the distance between the portent and what it portends diminishes to nothing' (*LE* 205) – a position that makes the '*triste* truth of realism' even more *triste*.

For Gillian, the most deeply pragmatic of the three and the one least distracted by questions of faith as she has chosen to 'manage' and to 'organize' her love and her marriage within the given context (*LE* 158), there is still the concern that one cannot run one's life, rather it runs you. Even she, however, trusts in a moment of truth. No myth or fable for her (the potentially portentous sign of the wedding ring does, to be sure, have 'magical' powers for Gillian, but these are only for 'warding off unwelcome approaches' (*LE* 206)), but rather the sublime possibility of unexpected human contact; a contact that annuls the individual before a force greater than him or herself – a force like god. This force is sexual, though none the less spiritual for that; in fact the description is among the most deeply spiritualized in the novel: 'I'm talking about something different, about that moment when someone is suddenly there, and says, without using the words, "It's me. It's you. That's all there is to say." As if some vast truth is being guessed before your eyes, and all you have to do is reply, "Yes, I think it's true"' (*LE* 206–7).

Oliver has no structure in which to place himself, and no hope of sublime incarnation. His concerns are local and the society in which he lives, despite its global aspirations, its intercontinental travel and its scientific advances, is local too, in the sense of being concerned only with its own moment and materiality. The world in which Oliver lives reluctantly, despairingly, is the world that Chris from Metroland accepted with such apathetic delight. It is the world inscribed in Barnes's first novel by the quotation from Bishop Butler, whom Oliver quotes without naming and calls 'Bastard. Old eighteenth-century bastard' (*LE* 191).

Stuart, without the explicit reference, also invokes Butler when chastising Oliver for making connections between disparate things. For Stuart this is a way of 'not looking at the world . . . Because it's only by looking at the world out there as it is and the world in here as it is that you grow up' (*LE* 158). So Stuart would appear to be linked, intertextually, with Chris and, therefore, to share his tired acceptance, his jaded complacency. This, however, is not so. First, Oliver is the one who explicitly shares Chris's position at the end of *Metroland*, when he states (perhaps for different reasons): 'But life does simplify itself, you'll find . . .' (*LE* 211).

Stuart is striving, every bit as much as Oliver, for meaning, for purpose, but his route to redemption takes a very different path. In part, Stuart attempts to provide for others, to be the distributor of good things. This is the case, however accidentally (as it should be, given the context), with the phrase 'the law of unintended effect' that Oliver picks up on, as well as the other more material generosity that he shows. The mixture of services that Stuart offers leads Gillian to take a term the girls have for him ('Just Stuart') and to imbue it with a denser, deeper set of associations concerning justice (*LE* 104).

Stuart, though, is seeking as well as giving. His goal is to win Gillian back, to reclaim love. The importance and/or failure of love has been discussed elsewhere, so I shall make just a couple of comments here in relation to Stuart's quest. As with the narrator of the 'Parenthesis' section of *A History of the World in 10½ Chapters*, Stuart does not any more believe that love will make you happy: 'Love leads to happiness? Come off it' (*LE* 172). More than this though, love as the sustaining principle of a structure of belief does not work either. Gregory in *Staring at the Sun* had stated that God does not need to be just, God only needs to be true. Stuart, lacking a god, places love in its stead, but he discovers that, true or not, just or not, the attainment of your desires (the fulfilment of your belief) is not an end, it does not provide contentment or relief. Braithwaite in *Flaubert's Parrot* had paraphrased Larkin to ask about the wisdom of rushing into fulfilment's desolate attic. Here, Stuart states that, when 'things were impossible, they were clearer' (*LE* 249). Lacking or gaining truth, living with or without gods or their substitutes: neither position seems desirable.

Oliver seeks a disappeared world and can never be happy in this one. Mme Wyatt suggests this in a different context when, discussing Gillian and Oliver's marriage, she recognizes that Oliver will not be happy with Gill as the main wage-earner. Despite modern theories on equality between partners, she says, 'the modern theory is only good if the psychology of the person it is applied to is also modern, if you follow' (*LE* 90). And Oliver is not modern. He rejects science and business and is adrift in his mythological needs. Unlike Graham Hendrick in *Before She Met Me*, who, with terrible consequences, welcomed genetics as an explanation for life, as a sort of religious principle, Oliver recognizes but does not accept it: 'Nowadays we just tippy-tip our toes in the circus sawdust to the whipcrack of DNA. What is human tragedy for today's diminished species? To act as if we have free will knowing we don't' (*LE* 197). Barnes's novels have constantly probed the possibilities of 'today's diminished species', provoking questions about how characters respond to the modern world with its enormous growth in science and technology, its shifting political organization, the demise of old truths, and the formation of new ones. Barnes's novels are formally inventive, challenge questions of the true and the false, scrutinize history, dispute ideas of character and the self. In all of this, and, I expect and hope, in his novels and other writings to come, he is engaging in one of the profoundest aspects of contemporary cultural life: 'trying to find new certainties in a moral vacuum'.[4]

Notes

CHAPTER 1. INTRODUCTION: 'THE SONGS WERE THE MAN ...'

1. Julian Barnes, '1981' in *21* (*21 Picador Writers Celebrate 21 Years of Outstanding International Writing*) (London: Picador, 1993), 103.
2. Ronald Hayman, 'Julian Barnes in Interview', *Books and Bookmen* (May 1980), 31.
3. Julian Barnes, 'Tunnel', in *Cross Channel* (London: Jonathan Cape, 1996), 211.
4. Matthew Pateman, 'The Trials of Julian Barnes', *Leeds Student Independent Newpaper*, 29 Oct. 1993.

CHAPTER 2. STARTING OUT IN PARIS AND LONDON: *METROLAND*

1. Ronald Hayman, 'Julian Barnes in Interview', *Books and Bookmen* (May 1980), 30.
2. Frank Goodman, 'Growing up in Metroland', *Northamptonshire Evening Telegraph*, 24 Apr. 1980.
3. Auberon Waugh, 'Pseuds' Progress', *Evening Standard*, 25 Mar. 1980.
4. Bernard Levin, 'Metroland: Thanks for the Memory', *Sunday Times*, 6 Apr. 1980.

CHAPTER 3. THE HISTORY MAN: *BEFORE SHE MET ME*

1. Mark Abley, 'Watching Green-Eyed', *Times Literary Supplement*, 23 Apr. 1982.
2. The interested reader might like to know that Jack's figures suggest that 98% of men have masturbated at some time and that

96% still do, whereas Kinsey locates the maximum number at 85% and the minimum at 15% of men who have reached 55 and are married. I am unconvinced by both sets.

3. See Emmanuel Le Roy Ladurie, *Montaillou Cathars and Catholics in a French Village 1294–1324*, trans. Barbara Bray (London: Penguin, 1981), 173, 145, 151, for the quoted passages. The passage on page 173 has the misquotation.

4. It is noteworthy that Hendrick's euphemism is directly borrowed from Flaubert's description of the same process in relation to Louise Colet, a description that is presented to us by Geoffrey Braithwaite in *Flaubert's Parrot* (*FP* 53).

5. An interesting analysis of Hendrick as cuckold is given by Mark I. Millington and Alison S. Sinclair in 'The Honourable Cuckold: Models of Masculine Defence', *Comparative Literature Studies*, 29/1 (1992), 16. This places the novel in the context of patriarchy and suggests that 'hurt men' are dealt with badly in this system and this almost inevitably leads to acts of violence against themselves or others.

CHAPTER 4. SEEK, MEMORY: *FLAUBERT'S PARROT*

1. J. B. Scott, 'Parrot as Paradigms: Infinite Deferral of Meaning in *Flaubert's Parrot*', *Ariel: A Review of International English Literature*, 21/3 (July 1990), 58; R. Brown, 'Barnes, Julian (Patrick)', in Lesley Henderson (ed.), *Contemporary Novelists* (Chicago: St James Press, 1991), 79; Richard Todd, 'Confrontation within Convention: On the Character of British Postmodernist Fiction', in Theo D'Haen and Hans Bertens (eds.), *Postmodern Fiction in Europe and the Americas* (Postmodern Studies 1; Amsterdam: Rodopi, 1988), 120–2.

2. Andrzej Gasiorek, *Post-War British Fiction: Realism and After* (London: Edward Arnold, 1995), 159; Marina Vaisey, *Critics' Forum*, BBC Radio 3, 13 Oct. 1984, 5.45 p.m.

3. John Gross, 'Birds of a Feather', *Observer*, 7 Oct. 1984; Bernard Génies, 'Un anglais Flaubert et les perroquets', *La Quinzaine littéraire*, 1 May 1986; D. A. N. Jones, 'Irishtown', *London Review of Books*, 1–14 Nov. 1984; Michael Wood, 'Bovary and a Stuffed Bird', *Sunday Times*, 7 Oct. 1984.

4. Julian Barnes, 'The Giving of Offence', *Times Literary Supplement*, 23 Oct. 1981, p. 1128.

5. Julian Barnes, 'To Suit the Occasion', *Times Literary Supplement*, 3 Feb. 1984 p. 113.

6. Jean-Pierre Salgas, 'Julian Barnes n'en a pas fini avec Flaubert', *La Quinzaine littéraire*, 16 May 1986.
7. Francis Steegmuller (ed.), *The Letters of Gustave Flaubert, 1830–1857* (Cambridge, Mass.: Harvard University Press, 1980), 14.
8. Alison Lee, *Realism and Power: Postmodern British Fiction* (London: Routledge, 1990), 38–9.

CHAPTER 5. A HUNDRED YEARS OF SOLITUDE: *STARING AT THE SUN*

1. Richard Rayner, 'Everyday Miracles', *Listener*, 25 Sept. 1986; Anthony Thwaite, 'Heads or Tails', *Observer*, 21 Sept. 1986.
2. Carlos Fuentes, 'The Enchanting Blue Yonder', *New York Times Book Review*, 12 Apr. 1987.
3. David Crossen, 'Barnes "Sun" Story Fails to Shine', *Belfast Telegraph*, 3 Nov. 1986; Allan Massie, 'Barnes Goes Back to the Future', *Weekend Scotsman*, 11 Oct. 1986.
4. Probably the most famous account of the 'postmodern' in this sense is Jean-François Lyotard, *The Postmodern Condition: A Report on Knowledge*, trans. G. Bennington and B. Massumi (Manchester: Manchester University Press). While a difficult read for the non-specialist, it is an important, indeed seminal (and therefore much overquoted) book.

CHAPTER 6. FABLES, NOT THE RECONSTRUCTION: *A HISTORY OF THE WORLD IN 10½ CHAPTERS*

1. Andrzej Gasiorek would tend to support the view that this is authorial intervention, stating that the narrator 'surely speaks for the author here' (*Post-War British Fiction: Realism and After* (London: Edward Arnold, 1995), 163). A distinction between speaking *for* and speaking *as* the author needs to be maintained.
2. Kate Saunders, 'From Flaubert's Parrot to Noah's Woodworm', *Sunday Times*, 18 June 1989.
3. John Naughton, 'The Cut of his Jibe-Talking', *Observer*, 14 July 1991.

CHAPTER 7. YOU TALKING TO ME? *TALKING IT OVER*

1. D. J. Taylor. 'Fearful Symmetry', *New Statesman and Society*, 19 July 1991; James Buchan, 'An Unsuccessful Likeness', *Spectator*, 20 July 1991.

CHAPTER 8. AFTER THE FALL: *THE PORCUPINE*

1. Matthew Pateman, 'The Trials of Julian Barnes', *Leeds Student Independent Newspaper*, 29 Oct. 1993. The 'Related Texts' section of the Select Bibliography below lists details of where to find information about the political and legal events on which Barnes based his novel.
2. I. Dochev, 'Desires: The Erotica of Communism', in Michael March (ed.), *Description of a Struggle: The Picador Book of East European Prose* (London: Picador, 1994), 201.

CHAPTER 9. AN ISLAND OF THE TIME BEFORE: *ENGLAND, ENGLAND*

1. Penelope Dening, 'Inventing England', *Irish Times*, 8 Sept. 1998.
2. Andrew Marr, 'England, England', *Observer*, 30 Aug. 1998.
3. Dening, 'Inventing England'.
4. Maggie Gee, 'Julian Barnes: England, England', *Electronic Telegraph*, 25 Sept. 1998.
5. Dening, 'Inventing England'.
6. Andrew Marr, 'England, England'.
7. Lucy Kellaway, 'We Can't Do Business', *Prospect*, Oct. 1998, www.prospect-magazine.co.uk/highlights.kellaway.

CHAPTER 10. ENDING UP FROM PARIS IN LONDON: *LOVE, ETC.* AND CONCLUSION

1. Carl Swanson, 'The Salon Interview', *Salon*, 13 May 1996, www.salon.com/weekly/interview/960513.html.
2. BBC World Service interview, 13 Dec. 2000, www.bbc.co.uk/worldservice/arts/highlights/001213_barnes.shtml.
3. Robert Birnbaum, interview with Julian Barnes, *Identity Theory*, Mar. 2001, www.identitytheory.com/people/birnbaum8.html.
4. Matthew Pateman, 'The Trials of Julian Barnes', *Leeds Student Independent Newspaper*, 29 Oct. 1993.

Select Bibliography

WORKS BY JULIAN BARNES

Novels as Julian Barnes

Metroland (London: Jonathan Cape, 1980; London: Picador, 1990).
Before She Met Me (London: Jonathan Cape, 1982; London: Picador, 1983).
Flaubert's Parrot (London: Jonathan Cape, 1984; London: Picador, 1985).
Staring at the Sun (London: Jonathan Cape, 1986; London: Picador, 1987).
A History of the World in 10½ Chapters (London: Jonathan Cape, 1989; London: Picador, 1990).
Talking It Over (London: Jonathan Cape, 1991; London: Picador, 1992).
The Porcupine (London: Jonathan Cape, 1992; London: Picador, 1993).
England, England (London: Jonathan Cape, 1998; London: Picador, 1999).
Love etc. (London: Jonathan Cape, 2000; London: Picador, 2001).

Novels as Dan Kavanagh

Duffy (London: Jonathan Cape, 1980).
Fiddle City (London: Jonathan Cape, 1981).
Putting the Boot In (London: Jonathan Cape, 1985).
Going to the Dogs (London: Jonathan Cape, 1987).

Shorter writings as Julian Barnes

'One of a Kind' in Malcolm Bradbury (ed.), *The Penguin Book of Modern British Short Stories* (London: Viking, 1987).
'Shipwreck', *New Yorker*, 12 June 1989.

'Dragons', in Bill Buford (ed.), *Granta 32* (Basingstoke: Macmillan, 1990). Also in Giles Gordon and David Hughes (eds.), *Best Short Stories* (London: Heinemann, 1992).

'U', in Stephen Spender (ed.), *Hockney's Alphabet* (London: Faber & Faber, 1991).

'1981', in *21 (21 Picador Writers Celebrate 21 Years of Outstanding International Writing)* (London: Picador, 1993).

'Trap. Dominate. Fuck', in Bill Buford (ed.), *Granta 47* (Basingstoke: Macmillan, 1994).

Extracts from *Staring at the Sun* in 'Golf in Fiction', in Alec Morrison (ed.), *The Impossible Art of Golf* (Oxford: Oxford University Press, 1994).

Shorter Writings as Dan Kavanagh

'The 50p Santa', *Time Out*, 19 Dec. 1985–1 Jan. 1986.

Selected Journalism

'The Giving of Offence', *Times Literary Supplement*, 23 Oct. 1981, p. 1228.

'To Suit the Occasion', *Times Literary Supplement*, 3 Feb. 1984, p. 113.

'Unlikely Friendship: *Flaubert–Sand: The Correspondence*', *New York Review*, 10 June 1993, pp. 5–12.

'The Proudest and Most Arrogant Man in France: *Letters of Gustave Courbet*', *New York Review*, 22 Oct. 1992, pp. 3–5.

'Romancing Flaubert: *Rage and Fire: A Life of Louise Colet, Pioneer Feminist, Literary Star, Flaubert's Muse*', *New York Review*, 26 May 1994, pp. 12–16.

'Prince of Poets: *Selected Letters of Stephane Mallarmé*', *New York Review*, 9 Nov. 1989, pp. 10–14.

'Odilon Redon', *Modern Painters* (Jan. 1995), pp. 14-18.

Other

Volker Kriegel, *The Truth about Dogs*, trans. Julian Barnes (London: Bloomsbury, 1988).

'Preface' to Gustave Flaubert, *The Dictionary of Received Ideas*, trans. Geoffrey Wall (London: Syrens, 1994).

Letters from London (London: Picador, 1995).

Cross Channel (London: Jonathan Cape, 1996; London: Picador, 1997).

Something to Declare (London: Picador, 2002).

Julian Barnes Website: http://www.jbarnes.com. A truly excellent and well-run site. Well worth a visit or two.

CRITICAL STUDIES

Acheson, J. (ed.), *The British and Irish Novel since 1960* (London: MacMillan, 1991). An interesting general survey.

Adams, I., and Tiffin, H. (eds.), *Past the Last Post: Theorising Post-colonialism and Postmodernism* (London: Harvester Wheatsheaf, 1991). An interesting account of the rise of these two theoretical models, which tends to assert the greater political efficacy of postcolonialism.

Bernard, Catherine, 'A Certain Hermeneutic Slant: Sublime Allegories in Contemporary English Fiction', in Thomas Schaub (ed.), *Contemporary Literature*, 38/1 (Spring 1997). An excellent account of Barnes in this theoretical context – one of the best articles on him to date.

Bradbury, Malcolm, *The Modern British Novel* (London: Secker & Warburg, 1993). Brief but insightful account of Barnes placed in a useful literary context.

Brown, Richard, 'Barnes, Julian (Patrick)', in Lesley Henderson (ed.), *Contemporary Novelists* (Chicago: St James's Press, 1991). A brief, but thorough, account of Barnes's works up to 1991, with useful biographical information as well.

Earnshaw, Steven (ed.), *Postmodern Surroundings* (Amsterdam: Rodopi, 1994). A wide-ranging collection of essays concerned with 'the postmodern' in relation to literature, music, comedy, philosophy, architecture, and a number of other topics.

Gasiorek, Andrzej, *Post-War British Fiction: Realism and After* (London: Edward Arnold, 1995). A good short discussion of Barnes's works in the context of a number of other post-war writers.

Guignery, Vanessa, *Julian Barnes. L'art du mélange.* (Bordeaux: Presses Universitaires de Bordeaux, 2001). In keeping with the series, an enthusiastic and intelligent introduction to Barnes' work, especially good on the relation between realist and postmodern techniques. In French.

—— *Flaubert's Parrot de Julian Barnes.* (Paris: Nathan université/ Armand Colin, 2001). A complex and highly impressive analysis on *Flaubert's Parrot*. Aimed at graduate level students and written in French it is worth reading if you are seriously interested in delving deeply into the world of academic analyses of Barnes' work – it is among the best.

Higdon, D. L., ' "Unconfessed Confessions": The Narrators of Graham Swift and Julian Barnes', in J. Acheson (ed.), *The British and Irish Novel since 1960* (London: Macmillan, 1991), 174–91. A well-presented comparison of these two writers' narrative styles.

Humphries, Jefferson, '*Flaubert's Parrot* and Huysmans's Cricket: The Decadence of Realism and the Realism of Decadence', *Stanford French Review*, 11/3 (Fall 1987), 323–30. Interesting, if only to see how Braithwaite might fit into a decadent tradition.

Hutcheon, Linda, *The Poetics of Postmodernism: History, Theory, Fiction* (London: Routledge, 1988). A seminal book with a useful analysis of Barnes.

—— *The Politics of Postmodernism* (London: Routledge, 1989).

Kempton, Adrian, 'A Barnes Eye View of France', in *Franco-British Studies*, 22 (Autumn 1996), 92–101. An interesting response to *Cross Channel* with other references to Barnes's Francophilia.

Lee, Alison, *Realism and Power: Postmodern British Fiction* (London: Routledge, 1990). Another important book that looks at *Flaubert's Parrot*.

Moseley, Merritt *Understanding Julian Barnes* (Columbia: University of South Carolina Press, 1997). A comprehensive account of Barnes' writing to this date, including a useful section of his Duffy novels.

McHale, Brian, *Postmodernist Fiction* (New York: Methuen, 1987). Highly theorized account of what 'postmodernist fiction' might be. The division between epistemological modernism and ontological postmodernism seems a bit too formulaic to accommodate, for example, Barnes's work.

Massie, Allan, *The Novel Today* (London: Longman, 1990). A short book that gives very brief, but interestingly opinionated, accounts of a number of contemporary writers.

Millington, Mark I., and Sinclair, Alison S., 'The Honourable Cuckold: Models of Masculine Defence', *Comparative Literature Studies*, 29/1 (1992), 1–19. A rare look at *Before She Met Me*, which is interesting if not entirely convincing at times.

Pateman, Matthew, 'Julian Barnes and the Popularity of Ethics', in Steven Earnshaw (ed.), *Postmodern Surroundings* (Amsterdam: Rodopi, 1994), 179–91. A survey of Barnes's novels to this date that suggests that the popularity of the novels is due, in part, to their engagement with big ethical questions.

—— 'Philosophy in the Courtroom: Barnes, Lyotard and the Search for Justice', in B. Axford and G. Browning (eds.), *Postmodernity: From the Personal to the Global* (Oxford: Oxford Brookes University Press, 1996), 80–99. A discussion of *The Porcupine* in relation to Jean-François Lyotard's notion of political justice.

—— 'Is there a Novel in this Text? Identities of Narrative in *Flaubert's Parrot*', in Michel Morel (ed.), *L'Exil et l'allégorie dans le roman Anglophone contemporain* (Paris: Éditions Messene, 1998), 35–48. A discussion of the structural features of *Flaubert's Parrot*.

—— 'Precision and Uncertainty in *Flaubert's Parrot'*, in Antoine Capet, Philippe Romanski, Nicole Terrien, Aissatou Sy-Wonyu (eds.) *Flaubert's Parrot de Julian Barnes: 'Un symbole du logos?'* (Rouen: Université de Rouen, 2002) 47–58. An examination of the presentation of uncertainty in the novel, focussing primarily on the opening paragraph of the text.

Raucq-Hoorickx, Isabelle, 'Julian Barnes' *History of the World in 10½ Chapters*: A Levinisian Deconstructionist Point of View', *Le Langue et l'homme: Recherches pluridisciplinaires sur le langage*, 26/1 (1991), 47–54.

Scott, J. B., 'Parrot as Paradigms: Infinite Deferral of Meaning in *Flaubert's Parrot'*, *Ariel: A Review of International English Literature*, 21/3 (July 1990), 57–68. A complex and fascinating, if occasionally overstated, deconstructive reading of the text.

Shiner, Larry, *'Flaubert's Parrot*, Agee's Swan: From "Reality Effect" to "Fiction Effect"'*, Journal of Narrative Technique*, 20/2 (1990), 167–78. A not entirely convincing juxtaposition of Agee and Barnes, but a timely reminder of the too-often overlooked Agee.

Smyth, Edmund (ed.), *Postmodernism and Contemporary Fiction* (London: Batsford, 1991).

Stevenson, R., 'Postmodernism and Contemporary Fiction in Britain', in Edmund Smyth (ed.), *Postmodernism and Contemporary Fiction* (London: Batsford , 1991), 19–35.

Sullivan, Mary Rose, 'Julian Barnes', in Frank N Magill (ed.), *Cyclopedia of World Authors II* (Pasadena, Calif.: Salem Press, 1989), 132–3. A brief account of Barnes's work up to *A History of the World in 10½ Chapters*.

Todd, Richard, 'Confrontation within Convention: On the Character of British Postmodernist Fiction', in Theo D'Haen and Hans Bertens (eds.), *Postmodern Fiction in Europe and the Americas* (Postmodern Studies 1; Amsterdam: Rodopi, 1988), 120–2.

REVIEWS AND INTERVIEWS

Abley, Mark, 'Watching Green-Eyed', *Times Literary Supplement*, 23 Apr. 1982.

Astor, Judy, 'Shrink Needed', *Listener*, 6 May 1982.

Bayley, John, 'Time of Indifference', *New York Review*, 17 Dec. 1992.

BBC World Service interview, 13 Dec. 2000, www.bbc.co.uk/worldservice/arts/highlights/001213_barnes.shtml.

Birnbaum, Robert, interview with Julian Barnes, *Identity Theory*, Mar. 2001, www.identitytheory.com/people/birnbaum8.html.

Blishen, Edward, 'Growing Up', *Times Educational Supplement*, 2 May 1980.

Bragg, Melvyn, 'In Fine Feather', *Punch*, 17 Oct. 1984.

Brooks, Peter, 'Obsessed with the Hermit of Croisset', *New York Times*, 3 Oct. 1985.

Buchan, James, 'An Unsuccessful Likeness', *Spectator*, 20 July 1991.

Carey, John, 'Land of Make-Believe', *Sunday Times*, 23 Aug. 1998.

Cockburn, Patrick, 'I-Spy Things Unravelling', *Times Literary Supplement*, 21 Apr. 1995.

Crossen, David, 'Barnes' "Sun" Story Fails to Shine', *Belfast Telegraph*, 3 Nov. 1986.

Cunningham, Valentine, 'England, England', *Independent*, 29 Aug. 1998.

Curtis, Anthony, 'A Latter-Day "Jules et Jim"', *Financial Times Weekend*, 6–7 July 1991.

Davidson, Ian, 'Passing the Dummy', *Financial Times*, 29 Sept. 1984.

Dening, Penelope, 'Inventing England', *Irish Times*, 8 Sept. 1998.

Eder, Richard, 'Tomorrowland', *New York Tines Book Review*, 9 May 1999.

Fuentes, Carlos, 'The Enchanting Blue Yonder', *New York Times Book Review*, 12 Apr. 1987.

Fyrbank, P. N., 'If the French were Shorter in Flaubert's Day, did they Need to be Less Fat in order to be Called "Fat"?', *London Review of Books*, 4 Jan. 1996.

Gee, Maggie, 'Julian Barnes: England, England', *Electronic Telegraph*, 25 Sept. 1998.

Génies, Bernard, 'Un anglais Flaubert et les perroquets', *La Quinzaine littéraire*, 1 May 1986.

Glover, Stephen, 'Obsessed by Jealousy', *Daily Telegraph*, 15 Apr. 1982.

Goodman, Frank, 'Growing up in Metroland', *Northamptonshire Evening Telegraph*, 24 Apr. 1980.

Graham-Dixon, Andrew, 'Clinging to the Wreckage: The Craft of Julian Barnes', *Independent*, 24 June 1989.

Gross, John, 'Birds of a Feather', *Observer*, 7 Oct. 1984.

Hamilton, Ian, 'Real Questions', *London Review of Books*, 6 Nov. 1986.

Hayman, Ronald, 'Julian Barnes in Interview', *Books and Bookmen* (May 1980).

Hornby, Nick, 'Much Matter, Few Words', *Sunday Times*, 8 Nov. 1992.

Imlah, Mick, 'Giving the Authorized Version', *Times Literary Supplement*, 12 July 1991.

Jones, D. A. N., 'Foggy Girl', *Sunday Telegraph*, 21 Sept. 1986.

—— 'Irishtown', *London Review of Books*, 1–14 Nov. 1984.

Kaleidoscope, 16 Oct. 1984, Radio 4, 9.45–10.15 p.m.

Kakutani, Michiko, 'England, England: England as Theme Park', *New York Times*, 11 May 1999.

Kellaway, Lucy, 'We Can't Do Business', *Prospect*, Oct. 1998, www.prospect-magazine.co.uk/highlights/kellaway.

Kemp, Peter, 'Show Trial, New Style', *Times Literary Supplement*, 30 Oct. 1992.

—— 'An Author-ised Version', *Sunday Times*, 25 June 1989.

Kermode, Frank, 'Obsessed with Obsession', *New York Review of Books*, 25 Apr. 1985.

—— 'Stowaway Woodworm', *London Review of Books*, 22 June 1989.

King, Francis, 'A Fine Novelist, an Even Finer Writer', *Spectator*, 11 Oct.1986.

Kupfer, Steven, 'An Unsatisfactory Trip to the End of the Line', *Hampstead and Highgate Express*, 9 May 1980.

Lawson, Mark, 'Marmite for New Yorkers', *Independent*, 8 Apr. 1995.

Levin, Bernard, 'Metroland: Thanks for the Memory', *Sunday Times*, 6 Apr. 1980.

Lodge, David, 'The Home Front', *New York Review of Books*, 7 May 1987.

Mangan, Gerald, 'Très British', *Times Literary Supplement*, 19 Jan. 1996.

Marr, Andrew, 'England, England', *Observer*, 30 Aug. 1998.

Massie, Allan, 'Barnes Goes Back to the Future', *Weekend Scotsman*, 11 Oct. 1986.

—— 'Parrot with Many Voices', *Scotsman*, 13 Oct. 1984, p.18.

Naughton, John, 'The Cut of his Jibe-Talking', *Observer*, 14 July 1991.

Parrinder, Patrick, 'Sausages and Higher Things', *London Review of Books*, 11 Feb. 1993.

Pateman, Matthew, 'The Trials of Julian Barnes', *Leeds Student Independent Newspaper*, 29 Oct 1993.

Paxman, Jeremy, 'London Calling', *Sunday Times*, 9 Apr. 1995.

Rayner, Richard, 'Everyday Miracles', *Listener*, 25 Sept. 1986.

Rushdie, Salman, 'New Wave Ark', *Observer*, 25 June 1989.

Salgas, Jean-Pierre, 'Julian Barnes n'en a pas fini avec Flaubert', *La Quinzaine littéraire*, 16 May 1986.

Saunders, Kate, 'From Flaubert's Parrot to Noah's Woodworm', *Sunday Times*, 18 June 1989.

Shilling, Jane, 'A Trio for Married Voices', *Sunday Telegraph*, 23 July 2000.

Showalter, Elaine, 'Careless Talk Costs Wives', *Guardian*, 5 Aug. 2000.

Shrimpton, Nicholas, 'The Crocodile File', *Sunday Times*, 18 Apr. 1982.

Sutherland, John, 'Looking Back', *London Review of Books*, 22 May–4 June 1980.

Swanson, Carl, 'The Salon Interview', 13 May 1996, www.salon.com/weekly/interview/960513.html.

Taylor, D. J., 'Fearful Symmetry', *New Statesman and Society*, 19 July 1991.
—— 'Not the End of the Affair', *Sunday Times*, 30 July 2000.
Thwaite, Anthony, 'A Course in Creativity', *Observer*, 18 Apr. 1982.
—— 'Heads or Tails', *Observer*, 21 Sept. 1986.
Vaisey, Marina, *Critics' Forum*, Radio 3, 13 Oct. 1984, 5.45 p.m.
Waugh, Auberon, 'Pseuds' Progress', *Evening Standard*, 25 Mar. 1980.
Waugh, Harriet, 'Green-Eyed', *Spectator*, 17 Apr. 1982.
Wood, James, 'Bedizened by Baggage', *Guardian*, 4 July 1991.
Wood, Michael, 'Bovary and a Stuffed Bird', *Sunday Times*, 7 Oct. 1984.
Woods, James, 'Blinded by the Might', *The Times*, 24 June 1989.
Wroe, Nicholas, 'Literature's Mister Cool', *Guardian*, 29 July 2000.

RELATED TEXTS

Dichev, I., 'Desires: The Erotica of Communism', in Michael March (ed.), *Description of a Struggle: The Picador Book of East European Prose* (London: Picador, 1994), 189–201. Very interesting in relation to *The Porcupine*.
Evans, E. P., *The Criminal Prosecution and Capital Punishment of Animals* (London: William Heinemann, 1987). A fascinating book: many thanks to Julian Barnes for having brought my attention to it.
Gavrilov, V., 'Communist Party and Opposition Sign Key Political Agreements', in *RFE/RL Research Report* 1/14 (6 April 1990), 1–4. Useful background about Bulgaria for the historical context of *The Porcupine*.
—— 'Environmental Damage Creates Serious Problem for Government', in *RFE/RL Research Report* 1/21, 25 May 1990, pp. 4–11. Indispensable background to *The Porcupine*.
La Rochefoucauld, *Maximes suivies des Réflexions diverses, du portrait de la Rochefoucauld par lui-même et des Remarques de Christine de Suède sur les maximes*, ed. J. Truchet (Paris: Éditions Garnier Frères, 1967). Among these gems is the maxim that provided the inspiration for the title of *Staring at the Sun*.
Lyman, H. Etgers (ed.), *Eastern Europe: Transformation and Revolution* (Lexington, Mass.: D. C. Heath & Co., 1992). Also useful for information relating to *The Porcupine*.
March, Michael (ed.), *Description of a Struggle: The Picador Book of East European Prose* (London: Picador, 1994). Another good book to read alongside *The Porcupine*.

101

Musgrave, G. M., *A Ramble through Normandy, or Scenes, Characters and Incidents in a Sketching Excursion through Calvados* (London: David Bogue, 1855). The wildly surprising intertext for *Flaubert's Parrot*.

Nikolaev, R., 'A Year of Crucial Change in Bulgaria', in *RFE/RL Research Report*, 1/1, 5 Jan 1990, 7–11.

Paskov, Victor, 'Big Business', in Michael March (ed.), *Description of a Struggle: The Picador Book of East European Prose* (London: Picador, 1994), 214–17. A beautiful story that should be read alongside *The Porcupine*.

Savigny, Jean Baptiste Henri, and Corréard, Alexandre, *Narrative of a Voyage to Senegal in 1816; Comprising an Account of the Shipwreck of the Medusa* (London: H. Colburn, 1818). Interesting to compare this to the 'Shipwreck' chapter in *A History of the World in 10½ Chapters*.

Starkie, Enid, *Flaubert: The Making of the Master* (London: Weidenfeld & Nicolson, 1967). The book that causes Braithwaite such ire in its description of Emma Bovary's eyes.

Steegmuller, Francis (ed.), *The Letters of Gustave Flaubert, 1830–1857* (Cambridge, Mass.: Harvard University Press, 1980). Fantastic text in its own right, but also very revealing in relation to Braithwaite's narrative in *Flaubert's Parrot*.

THEORETICAL TEXTS

Barthes, Roland. *A Lover's Discourse*, trans. R. Howard (London: Penguin, 1978). Interesting to read alongside 'Parenthesis' in *A History of the World in 10½ Chapters*.

—— *Mythologies*, trans. Annette Lavers (London: Paladin, 1988). A seminal text in cultural interpretation.

Baudrillard, Jean, *Simulations* (New York: Semitext(e), 1983). Baudrillard is one of the most frequently referred to of the postmodern theorists. This brief selection is illustrative of some of his ideas, which in turn seem to be the basis for many of the theories espoused in *England, England*.

—— 'The Year 2000 Will Not Take Place', in E. A. Grosz *et al.* (eds.), *Futur*fall: Excursions into Postmodernity* (Sydney: Power Institute of Fine Arts, 1986), 18–27.

—— *The Illusion of the End*, trans. C. Turner (Cambridge: Polity, 1994).

Cohan, S., and Shires, L. M., *Telling Stories: A Theoretical Analysis of Narrative Fiction* (London: Routledge, 1988). A good account of narrative analysis that applies its ideas to a range of media, including literary fiction.

Connor, Steven, *Postmodernist Culture: An Introduction to Theories of the Contemporary* (Oxford: Blackwell, 1989). An often complex, but still intriguing and provoking, text that attempts to make sense of the broad array of competing discussions of modern world.

—— *Theory and Cultural Value* (Oxford: Blackwell, 1992). A difficult but often brilliant engagement with questions of ethics and value in the contemporary world.

Docherty, Thomas (ed.), *Postmodernism: A Reader* (Hemel Heampstead: Harvester Wheatsheaf, 1993). A comprehensive collection of essays and articles written by some of the most influential theorists of postmodernism.

Eco, Umberto, *Travels in Hyperreality*, trans. W. Weaver (London: Picador, 1987). Originally published in 1973 in Italy, this is one of the most readable and exciting of all the books that engage with questions that relate to postmodernity, from the author of two of the most successful 'postmodern' novels.

Fish, Stanley, 'Biography and Intention', in W. H. Epstein (ed.), *Contesting the Subject: Essays in the Postmodern Theory and Practice of Biography and Biographical Criticism* (Indiana: Purdue University Press, 1991), 9–16. Useful as a side text to some of Barnes's narrative strategies.

Lyotard, Jean-François, *The Postmodern Condition: A Report on Knowledge*, trans. G. Bennington and B. Massumi (Manchester: Manchester University Press, 1984). Probably the most famous of all the books concerned with the postmodern, it establishes questions of narrative as one of the fundamental areas of debate within discussions of postmoderntiy. The following books by Lyotard represent different aspects of his thought.

—— *The Lyotard Reader*, ed. A. Benjamin (Oxford: Blackwell, 1989).

—— *The Postmodern Explained to Children: Correspondence 1982–1985*, trans. and ed. Julian Pefanis and Morgan Thomas (London: Turnaround, 1992).

—— *Political Writings*, trans. B. Readings and K. P. Geiman (London: UCL Press, 1993).

Sarup, Madan, *An Introductory Guide to Post-Structuralism and Postmodernism* (Hemel Hempstead: Harvester Wheatsheaf, 1993). Does exactly as it says on the tin.

Waugh, Patricia, *Practising Postmodernism Reading Modernism* (London: Edward Arnold, 1991). An excellent attempt to provide readings of modernist texts in the light of postmodern theory.

Index

Taylor, D. J. 54
Todd, Richard, 22, 91

Verlaine, Paul, 5, 6, 8

Waugh, Auberon, 9, 25, 90
   Essays, Articles and Reviews,
   25

Winterson, Jeanette, 44
   Boating for Beginners, 44
Wood, Michael, 24

Zhivkov, Todor, 63

Recent and Forthcoming Titles in the New Series of

WRITERS AND THEIR WORK

"...this series promises to outshine its own previously high reputation."
Times Higher Education Supplement

"...will build into a fine multi-volume critical encyclopaedia of English literature."
Library Review & Reference Review

"...Excellent, informative, readable, and recommended."
NATE News

"written by outstanding contemporary critics, whose expertise is flavoured by unashamed enthusiasm for their subjects and the series' diverse aspirations."
Times Educational Supplement

"A useful and timely addition to the ranks of the lit crit and reviews genre. Written in an accessible and authoritative style."
Library Association Record

WRITERS AND THEIR WORK

RECENT & FORTHCOMING TITLES

RECENT & FORTHCOMING TITLES

Title	Author
William Hazlitt	J. B. Priestley; R. L. Brett (intro. by Michael Foot)
Seamus Heaney 2/e	Andrew Murphy
George Herbert	T.S. Eliot (intro. by Peter Porter)
Geoffrey Hill	Andrew Roberts
Gerard Manley Hopkins	Daniel Brown
Henrik Ibsen	Sally Ledger
Kazuo Ishiguro	Cynthia Wong
Henry James – The Later Writing	Barbara Hardy
James Joyce	Steven Connor
Julius Caesar	Mary Hamer
Franz Kafka	Michael Wood
John Keats	Kelvin Everest
Hanif Kureishi	Ruvani Ranasinha
William Langland: Piers Plowman	Claire Marshall
King Lear	Terence Hawkes
Philip Larkin	Laurence Lerner
D. H. Lawrence	Linda Ruth Williams
Doris Lessing	Elizabeth Maslen
C. S. Lewis	William Gray
Wyndham Lewis	Andrzej Gasiorak
David Lodge	Bernard Bergonzi
Katherine Mansfield	Andrew Bennett
Christopher Marlowe	Thomas Healy
Andrew Marvell	Annabel Patterson
Ian McEwan	Kiernan Ryan
Measure for Measure	Kate Chedgzoy
A Midsummer Night's Dream	Helen Hackett
Alice Munro	Ailsa Cox
Vladimir Nabokov	Neil Cornwell
V. S. Naipaul	Suman Gupta
Edna O'Brien	Amanda Greenwood
Ben Okri	Robert Fraser
Walter Pater	Laurel Brake
Brian Patten	Linda Cookson
Harold Pinter	Mark Batty
Sylvia Plath 2/e	Elisabeth Bronfen
Jean Rhys	Helen Carr
Richard II	Margaret Healy
Richard III	Edward Burns
Dorothy Richardson	Carol Watts
John Wilmot, Earl of Rochester	Germaine Greer
Romeo and Juliet	Sasha Roberts
Christina Rossetti	Kathryn Burlinson
Salman Rushdie	Damian Grant
Paul Scott	Jacqueline Banerjee
The Sensation Novel	Lyn Pykett
P. B. Shelley	Paul Hamilton
Wole Soyinka	Mpalive Msiska
Muriel Spark	Brian Cheyette
Edmund Spenser	Colin Burrow
Laurence Sterne	Manfred Pfister
D. M. Thomas	Bran Nicol
Dylan Thomas	Chris Wiggington

RECENT & FORTHCOMING TITLES

Title	Author
J. R. R. Tolkien	*Charles Moseley*
Leo Tolstoy	*John Bayley*
Charles Tomlinson	*Tim Clark*
Anthony Trollope	*Andrew Sanders*
Victorian Quest Romance	*Robert Fraser*
Edith Wharton	*Janet Beer*
Angus Wilson	*Peter Conradi*
Mary Wollstonecraft	*Jane Moore*
Women's Gothic 2/e	*Emma Clery*
Virginia Woolf 2/e	*Laura Marcus*
Working Class Fiction	*Ian Haywood*
W. B. Yeats	*Edward Larrissy*
Charlotte Yonge	*Alethea Hayter*

TITLES IN PREPARATION

Title	Author
Chinua Achebe	*Nahem Yousaf*
Fleur Adcock	*Janet Wilson*
Ama Ata Aidoo	*Nana Wilson-Tagoe*
Matthew Arnold	*Kate Campbell*
Margaret Atwood	*Marion Wynne-Davies*
John Banville	*Peter Dempsey*
Black British Fiction	*Mark Stein*
William Blake	*Steven Vine*
Elizabeth Bowen	*Maud Ellmann*
Charlotte Brontë	*Margaret Reynolds*
Robert Browning	*John Woodford*
John Bunyan	*Tamsin Spargoe*
Bruce Chatwin	*Kerry Featherstone*
Cymbeline	*Peter Swaab*
Anita Desai	*Elaine Ho*
Margaret Drabble	*Glenda Leeming*
John Dryden	*David Hopkins*
T. S. Eliot	*Colin MacCabe*
J. G. Farrell	*John McLeod*
Brian Friel	*Geraldine Higgins*
Nadine Gordimer	*Lewis Nkosi*
Geoffrey Grigson	*R. M. Healey*
Ted Hughes	*Susan Bassnett*
Samuel Johnson	*Liz Bellamy*
Ben Jonson	*Anthony Johnson*
James Kelman	*Gustav Klaus*
Jack Kerouac	*Michael Hrebebiak*
Jamaica Kincaid	*Susheila Nasta*
Rudyard Kipling	*Jan Montefiore*
Charles and Mary Lamb	*Michael Baron*
Roamond Lehmann	*Judy Simon*
Una Marson & Louise Bennett	*Alison Donnell*
Merchant of Venice	*Warren Chernaik*
John Milton	*Jonathan Sawday*
Bharati Mukherjee	*Manju Sampat*
R. K. Narayan	*Shirley Chew*
New Women Writers	*Marion Shaw*
Grace Nichols	*Sarah Lawson-Welsh*
Caryl Phillips	*Helen Thomas*
Religious Poets of the 17th Century	*Helen Wilcox*
Revenge Tragedy	*Janet Clare*
Samuel Richardson	*David Deeming*
Nayantara Sahgal	*Ranjana Ash*
Sam Selvon	*Ramchand & Salick*
Sir Walter Scott	*Harriet Harvey-Wood*
Mary Shelley	*Catherine Sharrock*
Charlotte Smith & Helen Williams	*Angela Keane*
Christopher Smart	*Neil Curry*
Stevie Smith	*Martin Gray*
R. L. Stevenson	*David Robb*
Gertrude Stein	*Nicola Shaughnessy*
Bram Stoker	*Andrew Maunder*
Tom Stoppard	*Nicholas Cadden*

TITLES IN PREPARATION